T0368740

INCIDENT AT HANOI

MADAMBA PRODUCTIONS LLC

Order this book online at www.trafford.com
or email orders@trafford.com

Most Trafford titles are also available at major online book retailers.

© Copyright 1994, 1998, 2005 Madamba Productions LLC.
All rights reserved. No part of this publication may be reproduced, stored in a retrieval
system, or transmitted, in any form or by any means, electronic, mechanical, photocopying,
recording, or otherwise, without the written prior permission of the author.

The copyright for the underlying work was registered as follows with the United States Copyright Office:
Original Registration: 31 October 1994
Derivative Work Registration: 6 July 1998.

The above-referenced works and rights to all derivative works
were subsequently assigned to Madamba Productions LLC.

Printed in the United States of America.

ISBN: 978-1-4120-5975-6 (sc)
ISBN: 978-1-4669-7932-1 (e)

Trafford rev. 01/10/2013

 www.trafford.com

North America & international
toll-free: 1 888 232 4444 (USA & Canada)
phone: 250 383 6864 ♦ fax: 812 355 4082

Table of Contents

Prologue

by SFC Michael Thompson, USA Retired

I consider it an honor to write the prologue for this exposé of a classified mission into North Vietnam in December 1966. I consider the author, Dale H. Koski, a true American hero and friend. I first met Dale in 1982 with Jack Nelson, National Service Officer, Military Order of the Purple Heart. I was and still am the Adjutant of the Chapter Dale joined. Jack remarked that Dale had the most impressive discharge he had ever seen (and Jack saw thousands).

My first impression of Dale was as a stereotypical Marine, with hair in the typical gung-ho fashion. I myself served in the Corps from 1957 to 1961. Talking to Dale, I found out he was a Recon Marine, Elite of the Elite. Over the years; I have heard Dale tell the story of Operation Snafu countless times, never bragging, in a straightforward and honest manner. Our country will never admit to the operation, because it led to the slaughter of POWs. After this mission, Dale was nominated for the Medal of Honor and three Purple Hearts to go with the three he already had.

In 17 years of working with veterans, I have never met one who has bled more and been screwed over more by our government than Dale. When he applies to the U.S. Department of Veteran Affairs for compensation for medical and physical disabilities he incurred on this operation, he is always denied, despite the evidence. I believe this book will be a cleansing for Dale and veterans everywhere.

Chapter 1

I was born May 23, 1944, in Bemidji, Minnesota. My father and his brother were in the Army overseas, locked into battle with the Germans. He and his brother were together there. It was somewhere in Italy, I think.

I was told by my older brother later that our relatives used to come over for dinners, and talk about the war, of course. My mother's three brothers were in the Army as well. Two of them were in the Pacific, one in the Philippines. All of my grandparents were waiting for Bud to return, but he was never seen alive again. When it gradually dawned on all our relatives and friends that he wasn't coming back, they somehow accepted it. War, and its dead and wounded, are not forgotten. Bud was killed at Bataan.

I started kindergarten in Duluth, Minnesota. I completed the first grade and then I moved to San Francisco, California, with my older brother Don and my mother and father. After we got there, my younger brother Duane was born, on May 22nd, 1948. Don joined the Marines and was shipped to the East Coast for his training. He wrote to us as much as he could.

Meanwhile, I was going to school in San Francisco. My sister, Ria, was attending her first year of high school at Mission High. I was at Bessie Carmichael Elementary School and eventually attended Francisco Middle School. My mother and older cousin Jane were killed in an automobile accident. The Red Cross notified my brother, and he came home on emergency leave. My Aunt Elizabeth was taking care of Duane, who was only a baby. It was very hard on us, especially during the funeral, where we found ourselves motherless.

My Aunt Elizabeth and Uncle Jimmy, who was also an ex-captain in the Army, were always very nice to us. We lived on Anza Street in San Francisco.

My mother's death led my father to a drinking problem. He would get drunk and beat us almost every night.

We finally moved from his house—actually, he threw us out. Our aunt and uncle took us in.

From the first day that I arrived, I ran into trouble in the form of the second oldest boy named Gene. He was meaner than a hornet and I worked with him feeding cattle hay. This was in the winter—it was terrible, miserable, snowy, wet weather. Gene was always in a bad mood, and we were always outside all day. He was about ten years older than me.

Sometimes they would let me go to a country school. I rode to school on horseback—everywhere we went, we traveled on horseback. I finally graduated from the eighth grade.

Over the next few years, I worked on several ranches. I finally returned to San Francisco where I attended Mission High School. I competed in swimming and played a lot of football, and I lettered in both.

My sister and my aunt looked after us. My uncle Jimmy went to South America, where he worked for Firestone Tire Company. He was always sending us pictures of large snakes that he encountered while working.

My sister was married to a Jewish guy, and they ran

a store in Washington, D.C.. He was a piano player and one night when he was returning from a band session, a car hit him, and kept on going. He was found dead. They had one girl named Liza. My sister married another guy named Bob, and they raised four more kids. They moved to Maryland, and about this time I was out of school and up for the draft. After some thought, I said to myself, "Why not join the U.S. Marines?" I had one older cousin who had been a Marine during Tarawa, and one cousin, on my mother's side, who had fought with the Army in Germany.

I thought of getting one up on the draft board, so I went down and took the test. The recruiter's office passed me in everything, so the next step was getting on a plane to Jacksonville, Florida. I got another physical there, then I was off to Parris Island, South Carolina.

I guess none of us knew what to expect as we got off the plane and started to board the trucks. The first thing we heard was, "You are not a civilian, you are not a Marine, you are the lowest form of life on the planet." With this being said to us, we saw our drill instructors coming at us. Instead of boarding the trucks, we were all down in the push-up position, and after countless push-ups, we were ordered to recover our suitcases and fall in at attention. Soon the motors on the truck started, but we weren't on them. Instead, we ran ahead and along the side and behind our drill instructors. They seemed to enjoy this. If anyone looked tired, he was selected to run around the entire grounds including the trucks.

We must have run about five miles when we were ordered into the leaning rest position. After another long session with jumping jacks, we were in the trucks and in about five minutes, we entered the gates of Parris Island, South Carolina, Recruit Training Base.

As we dismounted from the trucks, our drill instructors pulled the end gate out from under us, and we went spilling onto the cement parade field—one on top of the other. I had no idea I could get so tired so fast.

We were marched into ranks and files, and stood half

the night waiting to get assigned to whatever platoon they wanted us in.

I was assigned to Platoon 222, 2nd Battalion, MCRD. The next thing we knew, we were headed in for haircuts, showers, and issued basic equipment. We were then issued locker boxes for our gear. This went on all night long, no sleep until about three a.m.. We then made up our racks with sheets and blankets, and piled into bed.

One hour later, reveille was sounded, and we all hit the deck to start the day at four a.m.. We quickly dressed and ran to breakfast, which consisted of "shit on a shingle" and milk. After a very hasty breakfast, all of four to five minutes, we all stood up, shaved heads, confused, thinking again, "What did I get myself into?" We scraped off our trays into the shit cans and fell in outside the mess hall.

Well, we all looked pretty funny in our brand new green herringbone utilities, boon dockers, and crumpled up utility caps. The first week went by fast. We were getting shots in our arms for everything from flu to typhoid. We saw sick bay for all our needs—the Navy corpsmen and doctors held us in contempt.

We were not Marines, we were only recruits, and they let us know it. The second week, we were forming a platoon in big trouble. Every morning our mattresses, sheets, blankets, and racks were tipped all over the deck. The floors were called decks, the walls were called bulkheads, the ceiling was the overhead, the bathrooms were heads, the hallways were passageways, the doors were hatches, the drinking fountains were scuttlebutts, the windows were ports, a bed was a rack. You never sat on your rack, you sat only on the locker box. Anyway, every morning we were jarred awake by terrible noises. It would be 3:30 a.m., and the drill instructors would be pushing and knocking the double tiered racks over. The man on the top rack would have a nasty fall if he was still asleep.

When they sounded reveille, it would be blaring through very loud speakers, played by record. The end of the second week we were marched down to the armory and were issued our new M-1 rifles. They were all bathed in cosmoline grease to prevent rust and corrosion.

We were also issued our 782 gear, consisting of bayonet and bayonet scabbard, one web green adjustable belt, and M-1 cartridge pouches (six in all).

Our platoon spent the whole morning cleaning our rifles. We had also been issued cleaning gear consisting of a 4-piece .30-caliber cleaning rod, cleaning patches, and oil. After we had cleaned our rifles, we fell into formation, and the drill instructors inspected the rifles.

Needless to say, we did not pass the inspections, and we duck walked back to the company area, making duck noises all the way. Walking like a duck gets very tiresome after a short while.

The next morning, the house mouse, (that's the name for the recruit who aids the drill instructors at night), came in and whispered to me that the drill instructors would come in early and throw sand all over our rifles, which were neatly stacked and locked into rifle racks. There were three rifle racks, all painted olive green, one rack at each end of the building and one in the center. Sure enough, here came the two junior drill instructors with one bucket of sand each. They threw sand on every rifle.

At reveille we always used two men to make the rack together, got dressed, and fell out in formation at attention. The senior drill instructor or, most of the time, the junior drill instructor, would give us the order for double time around the "grinder", nickname for the parade field. We wouldn't get a chance to relieve ourselves until this was done four times.

We would then return to the barracks, secure our rifles in the rifle racks, leave one man back as security—called a firewatch—and double time to chow call. As soon as chow call was completed, we ran in formation back to the company area. If you caught firewatch during the night, you could be pretty tired the next day because no matter what happened, you still completed the drills with everyone else.

A normal day in the U.S. Marine Corps as a boot recruit generally consisted of being awakened at 3:30 a.m., making racks, getting dressed, grabbing your rifle, running to the grinder, getting into formation, running top speed with rifles at port arms around the grinder at least twice, returning to barracks, securing your rifle and 782 gear into lockers, falling into formation, and running to chow. Everywhere a recruit went, he ran double time. After the head calls, we field dayed the whole area, started cleaning rifles, washed our clothes with a scrub brush at a scrub concrete platform, which was about waist high with several water faucets each about thirty-six inches apart. After that, we would hang our clothes up to dry. One recruit was left for security. After that came COD (close order drill). Every day in the blazing sun we were taught how to dress it up, align ourselves with each other, and become ranks and files doing the rifle manual, port-to-arms inspection arms, order arms, trail arms, and left-shoulder arms, and right-shoulder arms.

We and our rifles got to know each other very well. After COD came running ropes over every kind of obstacle known to man, and always with our newly issued backpacks, ponchos, rifles, and 782 gear.

After that, we did double time to the chow hall, stacked arms, and filed into the chow hall. We had about ten minutes to eat, depending on which file or side went in first. If you were unlucky enough to be the last file, you might have five minutes. In the afternoon, it was learning how to present arms and the rest of the rifle manual at 1500 hours or 3:00 p.m.

We were being instructed in the fine art of bayonet training. Two recruits would fall out and face each other with pugil sticks; they would train on butt strokes and vertical and horizontal strokes. Generally, one or the other was unprepared. If you didn't want to be aggressive, the DI would make you fight two at once, until they really beat the hell out of you. Everybody was taught that the U.S. Marines, with rifle and bayonet, were America's most terrible weapons.

This was the next to the last thing toward the end of the afternoon. We would double-time to the swimming pool for drown proofing, which meant spending one hour in the pool with equipment and uniforms on. This was taught in case the ship went down, or you fell off a wet net while boarding your peter or mike boat. It would help save your life. One good thing my father did was teach me how to swim. It saved my life later. After so many laps around the pool that you thought you were a fish, we changed clothes and ran to the mess hall. After we ate, the DI's would say the smoking lamp was lit. It meant that whoever had a smoke could light up. We then double-timed to the barracks. Sometimes we were allowed to clean our rifles or sit on our locker boxes and get out a fast letter on USMC stationery. But most of the time it would be indoor smoker fist fighting whoever the DI's designated. They would pick out two recruits at random and throw them in the shower naked and tell them to try and kill each other. Here I was lucky again—my father had created a killer instinct in me.

Good old Sunday routine: if you wanted, there was the chapel, so at five a.m., after breakfast, we finished cleaning our living area and stood by for church call at seven. All denominations went to the chapel at one hour after another, so by ten o'clock, church was over and we, as stragglers, returned to our area. The rest of the morning, we were allowed to sit on our footlockers to study our guide books and learn our rifle parts by heart. As 11:30 approached, we fell out for chow. At least on Sunday we had a full twenty minutes to eat. What a luxury! Right after we returned from the mess hall, we were informed that we would take part in organized grab ass, so Pvt. Smith, my bunk mate asked, "What the shit is grab ass?" We all changed into physical fitness gear and tennis shoes, and waited. At 1 p.m. on the dot, the drill instructors announced it was time for 1300 grab ass.

We fell out into formation and as we double-timed

down to the big sea-shell covered field I saw large muscular individuals, all standing at parade rest about the same size group as us. We found out that these people had been on the island fifteen weeks and they were ready to graduate next Friday.

We also found out that they had been on this same grab ass field fifteen times in the last fifteen weeks. We were just a forming platoon and had fifteen more weeks ahead of us. The first thing our drill instructors said to us was, "Get out there and kick ass, hurt them, put them in sick bay so they can't graduate!" If you got hurt during grab ass, you would get set back two more weeks to the next upcoming platoon, and that was considered a disgrace.

So everyone was mentally prepared not to get hurt. The first thing we heard as we stood and faced the other platoon from 3rd battalion was that 2nd battalion was not even capable of fighting women. When we heard this catcall chanting, the DI's called us out by the numbers. When my name came up, I ran to the middle of the field, the other man from the opposite side of the field was running right at me and we both reached the 100-pound sandbag at the same time. I threw a body block at him and we both went down. I grabbed the sandbag and started to our side when I was tackled from behind by another person, so then one more of our platoon came out to help me fight off the second person. And so it went. Whoever carried the sandbag back to his side received a point for that side. Even though they were bigger, stronger, and had been training for all those weeks, we still mauled them. Our DI's were proud of us, but didn't show it.

Now for the fine art of marching and slapping at sand fleas. Slapping a sand flea was not tolerated, especially if one was at rigid attention when a Parris Island sand flea landed on your neck and started biting you. If the DI saw the offender slapping one, they were in for a dose of extra push-ups and whatever else they decided to punish you with. Sometimes we had sand flea burials. You would have to dig a hole, six feet by three feet, bury the flea and, sometimes, dig him up again.

As time went on, we got to know each other in our platoon, but there were never any loud conversations, just a few words spoken when the DI's weren't looking. Slowly, we became a good platoon.

After eight weeks, we were on the rifle range snapping in with our M-1 rifles practicing the sitting, kneeling, standing, and prone positions. After one week of snapping in on targets, everybody's arms and joints were very sore from stretching every limb to the limit. Come our second week, we were live-firing at targets, as we fired rapid and slow fire and learned how to adjust our windage and elevation knobs. Pretty much all hands were getting on to how to hit a target on bull's-eye at 500 yards in the prone position with 8 rounds, and at the 200- and 300-yard distances, we came out with a lot of bull's-eyes. Overall, at the end of qualification day we had 87 percent expert shooters, with the other 13 percent being sharpshooters and marksmen. Our Series 221-222-223 Platoons had one of the highest averages for recruit shooting, we pasted a lot of bullet holes over, and worked in the target butts.

When we were not shooting, the rifle range was a relief from the everyday grind. We, as a platoon, all were required to fire the Bar-Browning automatic rifle, the .30-caliber machine gun, and the .45 pistol for familiarization.

After we left Elliot, we returned to the barracks and soon found out we were in for some extensive hand-to-hand fights with a knife, against a Sgt. Nadeau who took it on himself, as our instructor, to teach us all we could learn in three weeks about how to stay alive while fighting a knife, bayonet, club or even machete. We picked up the general idea.

Finally, our platoon went to Elliot's beach where we learned how to walk a post and pull guard duty. In our fifteenth week, we got word we were having a final field inspection, so we had our uniforms pressed, brass shined, shoes polished, and rifles cleaned, in order to get ready to graduate from the island.

Well, I was a right guide who carried the platoon colors, so I expected to graduate as a PFC (Private First Class). No such luck. I left the island a private (PVT). But when the last day came around, I was more than happy just to leave. We had no poggy bait (candy gum), no flicks, no slopchutes (beer bars), or any place serving alcohol, for sixteen weeks, and it was now the middle of August and a long hot summer the day before graduation.

We received our (MOS) Military Occupation Specialty. I got an 0331 Machine Gunner Specialty. Anything with 03 meant Infantry, 0300 was Rifle Man, and so on. The Marine Corps must have needed us because almost the whole lot of us were picked as 03's something or another.

Chapter 2

Suddenly we all got orders for 2nd ITR (Infantry Regiment) at Camp Geiger, North Carolina. Located at Camp LeJuene, North Carolina, the closest town was Jacksonville. Now all my friends and I were training our asses off with live-fire exercises and map and compass. Not to mention living with the copperheads, vicious poisonous snakes who made it a habit to crawl into your bed roll or poncho if you weren't careful.

North Carolina, land of pine trees and swamps. At least now we were called half-ass Marines. We called our female counterparts broad-ass Marines. After many forced marches, we finally got orders for a three-week leave. I had caught pneumonia at Camp Geiger, so I started my leave one week later than the rest of my Marine buddies.

I took leave to Minnesota and then I received orders for Camp Pendleton, California. The unit was called Kilo 3/5, 3rd Battalion 5th Marines. Their reputation as a fighting unit was famous from France to Korea.

On our flight to Camp Pendleton, we loaded up on three large planes. As we flew into camp, the plane in the lead clipped the top of a mountain, blew up, and caught on fire. We could see it out of our side windows; part of our original platoon from Parris Island was wiped out in a minute. When we landed at El Toro Air Base, no one would tell us anything. All I could do was look for missing faces. Anyway, we were trucked to Margarita, home of the 5th Marines. We got there early for once, and were assigned to different companies.

I received more equipment and a pistol, and they told me I was now an assistant .30-caliber Machine Gunner. My duty was to carry the gun. I had one Marine assisting me to carry the tripod, and one Marine carrying extra ammo. We were part of a rifle company, and we were called Guns. The rifle company was armed with M-1 rifles and Bars. We were backed up by H.S. Company headquarters and service-mounted on a flat vehicle frame called the Mule. They also had flame throwers, and numerous other death dealers, such as the .50-caliber machine gun. We also had battalion medical corpsmen assigned to us. Every time a bad fire broke out, there was a unit on loan at the local fire department to help fight it. Two tragedies happened. First the wind shifted and about one hundred Marines were trapped by the Santa Ana wind in a canyon and they burnt up. Then a truckload of Marines went over a cliff in the smoke, and about thirty men in all were killed.

Summertime in California can be desperate with dry weather and hot winds blowing, called Santa Anas. Whenever we caught fire standby, the whole squad bay shivered about the people who had been trapped. This was a hell of a way to die. The training went on, and we spent almost all our time in the mountains and hills of Camp Pendleton. We practically lived out at Casey Springs, a wild hilly terrain. The days would be very hot, and as night time slowly settled in, it would get freezing cold and I would be all sweaty.

Pretty soon the rains came and we were always soaked and cold. I caught another case of pneumonia and landed in the hospital. The only time we ever slept was on weekend liberty, sometime after equipment inspection on Friday afternoon when we had returned from the field. After inspections and liberty call had been sounded, I was just too tired to pick up a liberty card, and make it to Tijuana, San Diego, Los Angeles, or even Oceanside. Liberty was always something to look forward to, but sometimes I was so tired from no sleep all week, I could hardly keep my eyes open Friday night.

One Friday night after a grueling week of training, we caught Liberty call, (LIBO), and I hauled ass for good old TJ (Tijuana, Mexico). I had a hot date with a barmaid. Her name was Elena and she worked in a place called El Toro. When I walked in all squared away in my uniform, I was going to sweep her off her feet. But when I came through the door, I saw this sailor kissing her so I made some quick tracks to the bar and hit him so hard he did a back flop on the floor. Well, he must have come to fast, because he caught me from the back, and we fell out the back door. There was no stairway and I guess we fell, still struggling in each others arms, about three stories into some garbage cans. When I woke up, we were still laying there, he was out cold, but breathing, and I felt like every bone in my body was broken. Somebody called the Shore Patrol, so I took off. My uniform was in shreds, I was bleeding all over, and I really looked a mess. The last people I wanted to see were the Mexican cops or our U.S. Shore Patrol, so I took all the back ways to the border and slipped over. I caught a cab in San Diego, and hitchhiked on to the base. When the MP's saw me, I told them I was jumped by four civilians, they believed me and called the medical corps. The next morning I was sore, but very lucky to have no broken bones. The next weekend I saw Elena again, but she acted real nasty so I moved to other places to pull liberty.

TJ was a fun place, but very expensive on a private—I drew $39.00 a pay day, every two weeks. Money went a lot farther back then, but there was never enough to go around. On "base liberty" meant we didn't leave the base. We hit the local slopchute for a pitcher of beer and there were always a lot of fights. Everybody sat around and drank until they were shitfaced and had to low crawl back to the squad bay, where the fire watch had to see that they kept the noise down, and that there were no fights. Inside the squad bay, at 4:30 a.m., everybody had a terrible hangover. When we were in garrison, the name for the company area, which was rare because we were almost always in the field, we first field dayed (cleaned) the whole living area, then we took off over the ice plants and sidewalks to fall into formation and double-time to the chow hall.

After breakfast, we would straggle back to K Company area and prepare for inspection of all our fighting equipment, such as draw machine guns for drill and cleaning guns. Gun drill was always interesting. We would run up and down the hills, setting the .30-caliber on its tripod, firing at targets and going through the whole nine yards of humping the .30-caliber on force marching. We would work at guerrilla warfare, constantly improving our skills on ambushing other troops, setting up booby traps, and using trip wires with rocks in cans for warning us early that the enemy was near.

Sometimes we would have sleeping bags. If I caught any sleep, it would be with my .45 pistol always in my hand. California can be so hot in the day and so cold at night. I bet we only saw a rack to sleep in about twice a week, the rest of the time we slept on the ground, with ponchos and rubber ladies. A rubber lady was the nickname for an inflatable mattress 5 1/2 feet long, 3 1/2 feet wide and blown up by mouth.

K Co. 3rd Bn. was the perfect company. We trained constantly for capturing other unit prisoners. In the middle of the night we would sneak in and grab about four sleeping bodies, interrogate them and beat the hell out of them, so next time they wouldn't be caught by aggressors. We were picked for aggressor troops about 50 percent of the time. When capturing other unit troops, we sometimes caught officers, and we would really interrogate and rough them up.

When we weren't aggressors, we dug foxholes—fighting holes—and established a perimeter around our C.P. command post, which was where the Battalion Commanding Officer and generally the XO and 1st Sergeant were located. So we always had our hands full staying awake so we didn't fall from grace by being captured like everyone else.

Nighttime was a bad time for running into rattlesnakes, as well as daytime, for that matter. The snakes could be found sunning themselves and when disturbed, would actually come after you. And at night you couldn't see them, which made getting bit all the easier. We had a lot of tarantulas and they were always around stinging somebody. One night three of us ran into a cougar with cubs. The old cat gave us a warning not to come close, and we didn't. What a life a grunt Marine has!

We were always amphibious training, so we lived aboard ship constantly. Our living quarters were hammocks and a head, and we were always practicing the dry net. The dry net was a stationary story block that we practiced crawling down, simulating entering a Peter or Mike boat. There were gigantic ropes all braided together, with each space in the rope big enough for your boot and a handhold on the next square opening. On the rope there was always a Marine above you coming down, stepping on your hands, or you were stepping on the Marine's hands below you.

The dry landing net, as it was called, was made of hemp. It was stiffer then regular rope. After constant practice on the dry net, we started using a wet net, with four to six Marines over the side with rifles and field transport packs on their backs. They slowly made their way down to the waiting invasion craft below. In rough seas, the momentum of the troop ship first would pull you where you could practically touch the waiting barge below by reaching out and grabbing it from the top of the ship. The next minute the gravity force would pull you away from the landing barge as far as the ship could roll the other way.

We always unhooked our cartridge belts so if we fell into the ocean in between the ship and the invasion barge, we could swim for it until we were fished out. I saw six Marines fall and knock each other off the wet net, and three were never recovered. They always seemed to pick the stormiest days for amphibious training. We also did a lot of "hammer anvil" training. This was where the invasion craft covers the beach landing, and copters fly from a carrier and land troops behind the enemy, so as to push them into the invasion force. We did a lot of hammer anvil off the Valley Forge Carrier and wet net landing from the George Clymer and the other attack transport, the Noble APA 218. After landing one way or the other, we would eat our c-rations. These were highly portable canned rations, some of which needed heating before they could be eaten. We would make a bunch of holes with our John Wayne can openers that we carried around our necks with our dogtags, in the side of an empty can, and this was our stove. We then lit a thermo-heat tab and inserted it inside the cans and cooked our ham and lima beans, or whatever else needed cooking. We carried our c-rats in a black wool stocking so the cans wouldn't rattle. And then we prepared for another night of mosquitoes and no sleep.

I couldn't believe it, after two weeks of ship to shore, and hammer anvil, we got a weekend off. So I said to my good Marine Corps friend, Jack, "Lets go to San Diego and hit on the Waves or anything that comes along". That Sunday was the same day Marilyn Monroe was found dead, and we were on the beach listening to the radio.

All of a sudden we heard a shout and saw a guy's head going under. Well we swam about a block, and no guy, so we dove and, lucky for him, we got a hold of him. He was sinking in water about ten feet below us, I motioned to Jack and we could just barely see him. He was curled up with cramps and drowning when we got a hold of him. He started pulling my neck but we towed him in by both arms. He was just lucky we saw him in time.

He turned out to be one of our Battalion Corpsmen, I don't know what the hell he was trying to do, I guess he had a cramp. Anyway, one good deed done for the day, the rest of the day was all about Miss Monroe being dead. We were all heartbroken, as she was our main pin up. We went down to the U.S. Grant Hotel and got drunk.

As time went on, our training became harder and harder; we became sharper and sharper; honed to a sharp edge. Then I got the news that my Aunt Elizabeth had committed suicide by jumping off a bridge. No one could tell me why. She was driving a 1940 Chevy when she stopped her car in the middle of traffic, walked over and jumped off. They never found her body. It was a terrible shock to the whole family; she was like a mother to us.

Well, more training, wouldn't you know, night and day. Land navigation courses using the map, compass, and terrain features, calling in artillery on targets, using the map and grid squares for air strikes. I got stung by a scorpion, so I was hospitalized for a few days. I went to Los Angeles for the weekend and stopped into the LA USO. After that, I went to the Hollywood USO Canteen. You could dance there, eat doughnuts and drink coffee, or just sit around and listen to music. People also played cards, chess, or checkers. Those were the years, 1960-1962, carefree and heading into a good military career. I passed the test and made E-3, Lance Corporal, so I had a little more money to spend. Every time we had liberty, we had to donate one dollar to the United Way Fund, or we couldn't pick up our liberty card.

Sometimes when we weren't in the field training, we had Cinderella liberty, which meant we had to be back aboard base by midnight sharp. That meant if you didn't own a car, you better be on the ocean side bus. heading for Camp Pendleton, fast. If you were late getting back, you would find yourself standing tall, in front of the 1st Sergeant and then office hours by your XO or CO. This was called an Article 15 UCMJ, the universal code of military justice. The penalty was generally restricted to the CO area, maybe even walking extra fire watch at wee hours of the morning, or getting busted, losing a stripe, demoted, maybe even getting fined. Any of these things, or all, could happen for an unexcused absence. I was pretty lucky, I only had some minor offenses.

It was the fall of 1962. Castro and the Russians had plans for missile sites aimed at the United States, we got the red alert and we packed up all our gear and stood ready at White Beach in Del Mar, California. Within hours we were on the USS Noble APA 218 and on our way to Cuba by way of the Panama Canal. Every night we steamed darkship in a convoy and we all sensed something was up.

During the day we fired our new NATO 7.62 millimeter machine guns off the side, and got familiar with the

17.

new gun—our .30 calibers were obsolete. The new M-14 replaced the M-1 rifle. The M-14 was a beautiful rifle, it had a 20-round magazine, compared to the M-1 rifle's 8-round clip. Don't get me wrong, the M-1 rifle is a jewel for accuracy, but the M-14 was also very accurate. We also received the M-79, nicknamed the blooper. It was a break-open shotgun type grenade launcher with a short barrel and very deadly on groups of troops.

By this time we were familiar with the swabbies, the Navy that ran the ship. Our title was FMF, Fleet Marine Force, or so lovingly called, Fighting Mother Fuckers of the Fleet. As we steamed down the Mexican Coast into Central American waters, we picked up more ships in our convoy. You couldn't see a light on any ship, as far as you looked. In my company we were now Charlie one seven.

We had some 2nd World War veterans from Tarawa and Iwo Jima, and a large number of Korean war vets. They told us a lot of tricks they had learned fighting the Japanese, North Koreans, and Chinese. During the day on board ship, we had plenty of physical training to keep in shape, and all kinds of weapon inspections. Once in a while they would put on a (smoker) boxing match, between us and the Navy. We had plenty of fights with the Navy as it was. They gave us the impression we were crowding them off their own ship, but for the most part, we all got along.

As we entered the Panama Canal, it was a slow process getting through the locks onto the Eastern side from the Pacific to the Caribbean Sea, and we were a few days doing it. Meanwhile, the only pleasures we had were the Gee dunk ice cream parlor and some state room movies. As our fleet entered the Caribbean Sea, one could see thousands of ships. In some ways it was comparable to the Normandy Beach Landing 17 1/2 years earlier.

We floated around for weeks, same old routine PT, hand-to-hand combat, firing weapons over the side and then cleaning our weapons. We also had Spanish classes, as we practiced all military words in Spanish. We were lucky to have some Marines who were from Spanish speaking families, so we learned firsthand some important words. As President Kennedy and the Russians talked, we neared zero hour. After what seemed an eternity, we got the word to stand by for wet nets. The night before, we began to get our fighting gear ready: we were issued grenades, C-rations, extra ammo, water, and all essentials for making war.

We were fully dressed and sitting on the deck when the ship's captain spoke over the loudspeaker. He said, "Now hear this, disembarking Marines, you will go over the side in ten minutes." By that time it was 0345 hours in the morning. Everyone was fastening their cartridge belts, and checking out their field transport pack to see if it set high on your back. Inside the pack was a tent, pegs, blanket, poncho, and all the gear with a rubber lady to set up housekeeping once on the Cuban Beach. There were also two canteens full of water, a first aid pouch, one .45 pistol and holster, .45 ammo on the belt, a K-bar fighting knife, and, on the right side, grenades hooked on pack suspenders.

We were all set. The rifle men were slinging their rifles over their right arms, and we were picked as the first wave to go in on the beach. So we climbed down the wet net into our waiting invasion craft. You could see the Coxswain roaring his motors as we finally loaded into our places. We put one bullet in the chamber and snapped the safe on, all riflemen fixed bayonets and we headed for the shore. Well, to our surprise, all invasion craft made large circles behind each other. This went on for about an hour, and as we looked over the side of the landing craft, we could see the sun glinting off their weapons. The hills and beach above us were honey-combed with God knows what all. Everything seemed to be shining. We started to take incoming bullets and mortars. The bullets whined off our front ramp. Lucky enough, no one was hit. We saw some artillery or mortar rounds splash close to us.

By this time, "When are we landing?" was on every-one's mind. They almost seemed to read our minds, and all invasion craft lined up for the first wave. We were just about in the surf line, when there was a gigantic flare that went up from the lead ships. The flares meant return to ship, invasion called off. Well, I couldn't believe my eyes! Little did we know, Kennedy had ordered the Russians and Cubans to begin to dismantle their missiles.

About two hours later, we were all back aboard the good Noble and cracking jokes with the sailors about a near miss. I think the sailors were pissed off to see us come back intact.

Chapter 3

Liberty call, and some ships landed at different ports of call. Our ship landed at Kingston, Jamaica. We all had a glorious time there, getting laid five times a day by five different women. We also drank a boat load of rum and visited the different cafes. What a life! We then left and steamed for the island of Camp Garcia, Puerto Rico. There we made a training landing–the USMC was not to be cheated out of its landing. The surf was so bad there, the waves so high, 2 or 4 invasion craft were tipped over. There were at least eighty Marines killed in those stormy seas.

After we landed, we went through all the procedures. Puerto Rican people were riding by us on horseback, hollering hello to us. We pulled Libo call on Isabela Segunda, bought all their rum, visited all the local whore houses, and tore down a Cuban flag and burnt it. Then, after three more days of training, we set sail for the Panama Canal. At this time something else was in the wind. We didn't know then it was Vietnam. As we steamed back, little did we know some of us would be on this same ship again but in different waters.

The trip back to White Beach was a lot different than when we left it. We had ship movies on the top deck, and there wasn't that tension we had felt before; instead, there was a feeling of relief. We got back in time to take our Christmas leave. We went to San Francisco and had a ball, about thirty of us were from the Bay Area. Well, leave was three weeks, so when I reported back, my platoon sergeant said, "This outfit is going to the land of the rising sun. Those of you who are short timers, better re-enlist if you want to go where we are going."

During my leave, I decided to go to Minnesota, too, so I was there for a week and I saw some aunts, uncles, and old friends–including an old flame who was married. It was about thirty below in International Falls, Minnesota, so we didn't get to really travel to all the spots I wanted to see. I talked two friends into joining the Corps.

I was now a member of C Company, 1st Battalion, 7th Marines. The night I returned from leave, I was five minutes late, and the 1st sergeant jumped me out for not getting a high and tight regulation haircut. This meant clean shaven white sidewalls, (no hair on the sides of the head), and 1/4 inch high on the top of the head. Well, I was in trouble again, so when I was standing tall in front of the XO in the uniform of the day, which was greens, he said, "Your performance up 'til now has been spectacular. On the rifle range last fall you shot 228 out of 250, you are an expert rifle man, you also shot expert 45 on the pistol range, you qualified expert with the M-60 machine gun, and you're generally a pretty squared-away Marine. You are now a squad leader, and that' s a CPL, or sergeant's job. Yet, you are still a lance corporal." He then poured through more of my military history. He said, "You are credited with saving a drowning man's life and you made the Cuban detail. I can' t seem to find any black marks against you, but for reporting in late, and having an unsquared-away haircut, you are assigned to two weeks mess duty."

Boy, I really needed that! I worked two weeks in the pot shack, getting up at 2:00 in the morning and scrubbing and scouring large pots and pans all day till the mess hall was secured at night. This job was a back breaker, and the last day in the steamy interior of the mess hall pot shack, I vowed to not break any more rules. Plus, there was not even base liberty in mess hall whites, meaning the mess hall uniform. By the time we finished the mess hall, it was too late to shower and start a beer binge because of the hangovers a person would have at 2 a.m. Drunk and sick wasn't worth it, so I would drag myself the six blocks to my rack, to prepare for another day always putting on a clean pair of whites every day. Our mess hall gunnery sergeants would really pour it on the poor devils they were in charge of for the two-week period. At least one good thing about mess hall duty, I missed the cold nights in the field, and I didn't have to stand any weapon or equipment inspections.

That was left up to my second in charge, a PFC Evans from Chicago.

Whenever I saw him or any of my gun crew, we would compare notes. When I rejoined the ranks we started all night field problems again. It was really the greatest, running around in the rain and pitch black darkness. We thought we were the most professional hard heads in the Marine Corps. My last liberty in Los Angeles was almost a disaster. I met this girl at the L.A. USO and danced with her about five times. This was a Friday night and five of us just got off the bus from Ocean Side, California.

We all split up as soon as we got off the bus. I headed for the Roselyn Hotel on Sixth and Main. On the third floor was the USO for service people. Everyone there was very nice and you could always find some kind of meal, free of charge. This lady had been spiking her cola with gin all day and was about three sheets to the wind. She said to me, "Let's get the hell out of here, I have a room down the hall." I figured this was a good setup, because I barely had enough money to rent a room and eat the next day, and I was very tired from being in the field for five straight days. So we hit the pad.

Her room was huge with a big bed. She was so drunk she threw up on the floor and fell down. I had just gotten her in the shower and cleaned the mess up when there was a banging on the door. It was a guy who said the room was in his name and he invited this Judy to spend the night with him.

Well, she woke up about this time, and said she never laid eyes on him before. I saw the room receipt and her name was on it. This was some Air Force guy, so I told him, "The lady said she doesn't know you, so you're going to have to get lost." He tried to fight, but I beat him to the punch, kicking him in the head. He had to crawl out the door. The next day, Judy took off and I never saw her again.

L.A. was a fun place, and so was Hollywood. The USO there was another great hangout for service people, just like the USO in L.A. There were a lot of great people; we danced to Chubby Checker and Little Eva music. Sometimes we would get invited for Thanksgiving, Christmas, or just to parties. People were really laying out the red carpet for us.

Most of the older people were World War II vets, and twenty years before had lived the same life we were living now. Sometimes they invited us out overnight to sleep in their homes and have breakfast. They would mention they fought the Axis Forces somewhere between 1939 and 1945.

Life at Pendleton went on as usual, until we got the word that we were on the move again. One day at morning formation on White Beach in Delmar, we found out anyone with short time could ship over for either four or six years—meaning re-enlistment. Well, I had plenty of time left myself, so I knew I was going. As it turned out, just about everyone was qualified to go overseas. All of our gear was put on ships and the married men (brown baggers) all kissed their wives good-bye. Our new designation was Fox Company 2nd BN 3rd Marines at Pearl Harbor.

After visiting Hawaii for three days and stopping at all the Hotel street bars, the locals were glad to see us gone. I guess they thought we were going to take over the area. We had some good street fighters in our battalion, and got into six fights a night with the local bad asses. We always came out winners, and left a lot of broken fixtures behind. We drove the shore patrol nuts and even beat them up a couple times. They said we were a bunch of savages and drunks. F 2/3 was getting a reputation as something real special, like a caged tiger when he gets out.

The convoy's next stop was Okinawa. We unloaded all of our gear into cement barracks, which were very clean and shiny. Our new home was Camp Schwab, named after a USMC private who was killed in the battle for Okinawa. The area we moved into was very scenic, right next to the ocean. We had the same routine we had at

Camp Pendleton, (except this time no Casey Springs). Our new area of training was called NTA, Northern Training Area. Right next to our northern boundary was an Army radar unit.

We got to know them well and played sports against them at Camp Schwab. There was also 1st Battalion 3rd Marines, 2nd BN 3rd Marines, and 3rd BN 3rd Marines. We also had other components there, such as tanks, and everything it took to move out a modern fighting force as fast as possible aboard waiting ships.

We were always training. In the NTA we were always running into the deadly Habu, a very poisonous and aggressive snake. Once bit, you have very little chance of survival. We were constantly finding World War II relics, and even found a cave full of Japanese skeletons. Their rifles were workable, albeit somewhat rusty. From the skeletons it looked like they had died from flame throwers.

We had house boys at Camp Schwab, Okinawans who made their living shining our boots, shoes, and brass. They also pressed our clothes and cleaned our barracks. We didn't know how to act after doing all these things ourselves in California, but we made up for it in physical training exercises like running obstacle courses and weapon inspections.

We also pulled running guard, guarding many different areas of responsibility. Running guard could be a lonely job. If you did have serious trouble on your post, you relayed your distress call by field telephone, or vocally. If you were being stalked or set to be attacked, you shot first, with no hesitation. We had one post that was manned by the shore line fence between the camp's western border, the ocean, and the town of Henoko. At times people, Marines mostly, would try to sneak under the fence or swim around to get back to base undetected. They usually left base without a liberty card, and they weren't supposed to be absent from the base to start with. One night, one of our sentries shot a Marine dead when he wouldn't halt.

Everyone knew the sand dune route to Henoko. Under the fence, cross a few hills and you were there. Sliding doors, bedroom-eyed whores and plenty of opportunities to drink and fight. It was always more exciting to sneak into town without a liberty card. A two-dollar short time was always available, and generally every guy had his regular short-time girl. But if you went with another Naysan, the girls would soon find out about it, and call you "butterfly boysan". This could cause trouble with your everyday short-time girl. Every girl was always asking, "Will you marry me and take me to the States?"

I walked into a fight in progress one night, outside the Blue Moon Bar, and got hit with a large beer bottle (a Kirin beer bottle, I think). I got my left jugular nicked with glass. It required some stitches and I was in the hospital for a week. It might have been a blessing in disguise, because when I was at Camp Kuhue Army Hospital, one of our six by trucks missed a curve and went over a cliff. About 23 in our company were killed, and I would have probably been in that truck if I wasn't in the hospital.

This was June, 1963, and we had just returned from Mount Fuji, Japan. We spent a 90-day float between Japan and Korea. We landed just south of Pyongyang, Korea. It was the dead of winter, and snow was ass deep. They issued Mickey Mouse boots, extra thermal underwear, and parkas to all hands. The average temperature was ten above zero. We made an amphibious landing into an icy surf, and pulled a 45-day war game. The mountains were so tall, it took a day to crawl up them, and the hills were so steep you would take one step and slide back two.

When I was on a hilltop, I swear, you could reach out and touch the other hilltop, they were so close together, but if you wanted to reach the other hill, you had to crawl down a steep ravine with jagged rocks and small pine trees. We saw Korean cemeteries everywhere, built up in pagoda style, some with lanterns lit inside. Almost a forbidding place, we hardly saw anyone because they were inside staring out of their windows at us. We had six or seven MIG enemy aircraft buzz us, but no shooting, even though we were loaded up with live ammo. We were only a mile from the DMZ, and could see the Russian insignia real clear on their wings.

While on some high hills, we could see Chinese and North Korean troops just about on the other side of the No Man's Land between North and South Korea. The U.S. Army had some troops guarding the No Man's Land, and it was so cold we almost froze. We just couldn't keep warm, sleeping on a rubber lady with no tents. They were permanent personnel, we were just visitors. We were lucky to eat once a day. No hot food, just cold c-rations. Someone in S-3 forgot to include heat tabs to cook the c-rations with. How some officers earned their bars, I can never guess.

It snowed and sleeted all the time we were there. We were carrying M-14 rifles and they always worked good. If you kept your gas cylinder locking lug tight, your rifle would fire out 500 yards on the money. Well, wonder of wonders, we got the word to head for the ships. Some of us helicoptered to the carrier Valley Forge. Some of us peter boated back to the APA's and LST's.

We were so glad to see the last of Korea. The nearest liberty towns in Japan were just like Henoko; plenty of women and booze. One American dollar was 365 Japanese yen, so we exchanged our money while aboard the ship. The bar girls, however, preferred the greenbacks if you had them.

One Josan's name was Dragon Lady. She was about 6 foot 4, and built like a brick shit house. She would pick out a certain person every night, and one night she picked me. When I woke in the morning, I was hung over. She brought up a breakfast for me: rice, eggs, and saki. I hit the first bed I could find. It was a bean-bag pillow and feather bed on a floor of bamboo.

I was trying to get to Tokyo, but I got off the train at the rail head at Numazu, for what I thought would only be a few minutes. I got some saki and ran across some English-speaking Japanese. We had a big conversation about what happened to them some 17 years before, and as the night wore on, I got drunker and drunker. When I woke up, I was in this bed on the floor. All my money was in my pocket. In fact, they wouldn't let me buy a drink all night. I saw the woman who rented me the bed, told her thank you and left.

When we first hit Japan we were told not to play the conquering hero role. Some of the people I had talked to the night before were veterans of various island battles with U.S. Marines, so I had quite an experience with our former enemy, but everywhere I traveled people were nice and when I reached Tokyo, I got a cab and went to the Ginza. There, everybody was loaded, dancing and drinking. Not so much fighting, though, because the MP's were there in force. We had a big meal served to us at our table, and I didn't even know the other people there. If you wanted to, you could sit on the floor and eat. You took off your shoes outside before entering. It was considered discourteous to wear your shoes inside. There's no speed limit in Tokyo, so it's very dangerous to walk across the street. I reported back to Mount Fuji on time the next night at midnight.

We took all of our gear out of our big permanent tarpaulin tents and loaded it up, had our last beer brawl, and said good-bye to the Land of the Rising Sun. Our company boarded a flat bottom tanker and headed for Borneo by way of Guadalcanal. We stopped and made a landing there for more war games. After leaving, we were caught in a typhoon. We were walking the walls of the ship and almost sank. What a way to get back to Okinawa!

At any rate, we figured to return to Okinawa, but we pulled into Subic Bay at Olongapo, Zambales. We started seeing the rest of the FMF. Pulling into Cubic Point and into the bay, we heard that three ships out of our fleet had been sunk in the typhoon, with all hands lost at sea. It seemed that I was always in the right place at the right time. They put us on port and starboard liberty call, but we had to be back on board ship by midnight sharp. Cinderella Liberty is a might hard to pull when you're drinking San Miguel beer with a woman on your lap.

I ran into a female impostor (Benny Boy) my first night in Olongapo. I was sitting in the Seven Seas Bar when along comes this honey. She starts talking to me, and before too long says "Let's head for my pad, before you have to return to your ship." I said "Sure."

When we got to her room, I saw wigs everywhere, and guy's apparel. Not thinking too much about it, I crawled into bed with her and found out "she" was a guy. He had taped his penis to his belly to resemble a woman. All he had in mind was being intercoursed in the rectum. When I noticed this, he jumped out of the bed and grabbed a machete. I fought off the weapon, but it became very apparent to me that sooner or later, in my drunken condition, I would be cut badly. Well, as luck would have it, I managed to hit him with a chair in the dark and he fell out of the window and onto a low roof, without the machete. I got my gear on and left by the back stairway.

I just barely got back to the ship in time. The next night it was starboard's turn for liberty, so we on the port side stayed back. As the clock rolled down to 1300 hours, we were hitting the gang plank again towards town. I spent the afternoon with a lady named Daisy, a seamstress, who lived in Subic City. We took a jitney both ways, and I was late getting back to the ship, but one of our Fox Co. Duty NCO's logged me in one minute early, so no sweat.

The next liberty call, I went to Subic City again, but didn't find Daisy. I did run into one of her cousins, who cooked me a meal. Daisy finally appeared and they got into a big argument. Daisy accused us of sleeping together (she was right). By the time I took off for the ship, I was about 12 hours late, but it turned out almost the whole port side liberty was late.

So they held a Captain's Mast (office hours) for our whole group. I was up for E-4 Corporal, but my punishment was that I had to wait another year. Almost everyone else got busted (demoted), fined or both. Some people were secured in the brig. At least I didn't have to tear off my stripes.

I later heard from Daisy. She wrote me a letter from Quantico, Virginia, but I never saw her again. She wanted to bring her mother to the States, but she became an invalid during the war and refused to go.

We had two guys from San Francisco who were Japanese. During our first liberty, all people who were of Japanese descent were warned not to go ashore because of what the Japanese did 20 years before.

They went anyway, and the next morning, they didn't show up. Three days later, we found them in the Olongapo River with their hands tied behind their backs, beheaded. They were sent home in body bags.

Chapter 4

We just got back to the Rock (as Okinawa is referred to), and we were informed that all hell was breaking out in Vietnam. Some groups of people connected to the rubber companies had been killed. Some had been tortured first. We were assigned there as advisors.

We were all delighted to know that we would soon be going to Vietnam. This is what we had trained for. We thought we were the luckiest guys in the world. It was like we were the chosen ones. There was back-slapping and whoopees all around.

We were ordered to stand by for BN landing team orders. After the night before, I was hung over as usual. We didn't have any more off-base liberty, so no liberty cards were issued to anyone in the 3rd Marines or supporting elements. I just had to let the short-time Naysan Sachaco know what I was up to, so three of us ran the sand dunes gauntlet for the last time. She cried, said Buddha prayers for me and said, "Don't get killed or wounded, Butterfly." After an hour, I left and never saw her again. I heard she married a GI and went Stateside.

I returned to the base alone. It was about 0200 and there was a big yellow moon overhead. I slid past the sentry who was half asleep after I got through the wire. Back at our squad bay, I said my good-byes, I had sowed some wild oats, and was back at the barracks. Everyone except the fire watch was sound asleep, the duty NCO and the assistant duty were just trading sleep time for duty. The assistant duty was waking the duty NCO up.

The next morning, right after chow, we had a battalion-sized formation. Every swinging dick was there standing at formation. We got the word that Fox Co. 2/3 got the Noble APA 218. ACO 1/3 would attack by UH34D helicopters and other supporting troop carrying helos. This would be off the Valley Forge and other carriers available.

All night long, we loaded gear on every kind of ship. This was probably going to be a three-prong Hammer

Anvil. We rehearsed it probably 50 times back at Pendleton. Our air support was supposed to be Marine Corsairs and after inspection of all our gear, we moved aboard ship. Our squad even got its old berthing area, just like old times. We shot the shit with all our sailor friends, and the scuttlebutt was going around.

While aboard ship the next day, we were all informed to stand by. At the rear of the Noble, a loudspeaker came on and a voice said, "This is your BNCO. Welcome, Marines, you're on a worthy mission. It seems that where you're heading, there has been a terrible lot of Victor Charlie activity. Certain regions of Vietnam are being put into a state of terror because of the VC. The communists aim to take over all of Vietnam as we know it now. So far, they have begun a reign of terror, killing innocent people and destroying soldiers from the U.S. and other countries. You are going to find that you, as Marines, are bigger, stronger, and better trained with far more superior equipment. You have an edge on these people already. We want you to be aware that they will probably be fighting as small groups of guerrillas. So be aware of ambushing and booby traps. Above all, you will be supported by ship bombardment and air strikes against the enemy."

Well, we were happy to hear we had some naval gun fire to call in as needed. We were given some photographs of the various poisonous snakes we would soon encounter: krates, pit vipers, and cobras. We went into a refresher course on man-killing booby traps like the Malayan Bat Swing, and all the other deadly devices they had used against the Japanese, the French, and now us.

We didn't really worry about any of this, though. Oh, sure, we were concerned and all, but foremost in our minds was that we were here to kick ass and take names.

We made a quick study of all our support: aircraft, helicopters, and fixed-wing. We also got the word that the medical copters were standing by and that there would be plenty of reinforcements as needed. As the ship slid through the blue-green water and the shore got closer and closer, I knew that this was no exercise, this was the real thing.

The weather was so hot you could fry an egg on the deck. They named the operation White Eagle, and we studied enlarged maps of our aerial recon taken a short time before. It looked like jungle grew up next to the beach, real thick. At a distance, the white sand glistened and the sea was tranquil. The chaplain was topside to give services to all the guys of different faiths. The men that choppered in would hit into An Hoa and head south, with Marble Mountain on the northeast and Da nang on the coast. The rest of us still in Eye Corps would take on Chu Lai and Duc Pho, and some choppers would start the hammer pounding the anvil at Bongson in two corps. Our job was to land at Duc Pho. As we wet netted into the waiting landing barges, I thought of Cuba, just a few months before. I bet this was running through everyone's mind. We even had the same ship, the same naval crew, and the same barge. It was like a nightmare all over again. I just got completely over a case of pneumonia from the Cuban mission, and now I felt great except for the goose bumps all over. I wasn't alone in that, though. I bet most of the men had those.

We settled into the landing craft and they placed mortar plates and some machine guns down by the hoist, along with heavy boxes of ammo and c-rations. The Navy opened up with some heavy salvos in the area just ahead of us. There was a heavy cruiser running north and south, shelling the landing area. I was now a squad leader, so I was packing an M-14. My gunner had the M-60 and the ammo humpers were carrying extra linked-up ammo in cans. We were told our job was to intersect Highway 19 and Highway 1.

As we approached the waiting beach, the navy stopped its shelling, and we were ready for the landing. We started getting real heavy armor-piercing bullets, digging in and coming out of the ramp section. A few guys were already dead or dying. We no sooner hit the beach when out of the corner of my eye I saw a barge take a direct hit with a B-40 rocket. It looked like everybody was hit in a group. As we approached the bush line, three of us laid on our backs and watched the green tracers going by. You could get a manicure if your hands were up too high. I think we were pinned down there for maybe 30 minutes, with nothing to do but lay behind that log and pray.

Some Marines getting into peter boats offshore were getting point-blank 51-caliber and mortar hits right in the barges. Off to the side of the (GEO Clymer) APA artillery guns were being fired at them point blank. We were lucky as hell we landed first, or were we? Some of the LCV's were on fire and sinking. We were being fired on by a 51 heavy machine gun. It sounded like hail. On the way in, our platoon sergeant stuck a 45-caliber pistol at the Coxswain's head and told him to beach it. That was the last time I saw either of them alive. I knew as the landing craft slammed up on the beach, after a few of us jumped out of the barge, it took a direct hit inside. We were still crawling away from it, to the protection of some low ground and logs to hide behind. It seemed like more than an hour before we could start inching forward.

All around and behind us were wounded and dead Marines. All of a sudden they stopped firing and we engaged them in hand-to-hand combat. I was bayoneted in my left upper chest and right upper quadrant. I had shrapnel in both left and right hands, and a broken right wrist from shrapnel. My right elbow also had shrapnel. I was bleeding like a stuck hog. They were still dropping mortar rounds among our people who were laying there wounded or dead. There was a lot of screaming going on among the wounded. I think we killed about 75 dinks who were ahead that were shooting at us and rushed us with bayonets. We drew first blood and were still being attacked when we fought them off with our machine guns. One Marine raised up in front of me, he must have been shot clear through the head, because his blood in the air looked like Technicolor. The sun caught the whole scene like a picture. A grenade went off in front of us and three Marines were cut to pieces. At this time we were getting support from our ship's guns. Some naval gunfire was hitting low into our own troops.

The enemy finally fell back, leaving their dead and wounded. This was a Vietcong company and we wiped them out almost to the last man. Unfortunately, it cost us; our outfit was in sorry shape. I had shrapnel lodged in my buttocks, but I could still walk. They waited until night to come in and relieve us. A lot of people bled to death, I'm sure, and one of my friends being helped by a corpsman couldn't stop bleeding. Those who could still walk were airlifted to the carriers and later to the hospital ships. The Marines who relieved us plunged into the darkness of the jungle, and carried on the operation.

We later found out that this was a classified mission, and was not made known to the public at large. I guess they were all classified missions at this time. I mean nobody was supposed to be in Vietnam before 1964, according to all the bullshit the media was pumping out, and this was July 1963. I found myself being treated for all my wounds, mostly back at the Camp Kuhe Army hospital. We were decorated at the Camp Kuhe hospital, a brigadier general came in and presented us with the combat action ribbon. I got a Navy commendation with combat V clasp and two purple hearts.

We heard through the grapevine that the people who relieved us were doing a great job. I saw so many badly wounded people coming into the hospital. I heard a lot had been killed, but from what I gathered, the advisors were doing their job well as a whole.

On the way to Camp Kuhe in Okinawa, I ran into two old pals at the Saigon receiving medical unit. Later still, on the way to camp, we were at the U.S. Naval hospital at Subic Bay, and I saw more friends. I didn't stay in the hospital too long, though. As you know, the Corps keeps pushing you on. August 25, 1963, we were coptered into a raging battle. We landed in a really hot landing zone, coming in to replace other Marines. The bird was shot down and we all scrambled around in the high grass trying to get to our own perimeter. This was northwest of An Hoa. I got hit again in the hands, and was shipped to the hospital ship Repose. I had shrapnel in both hands, and still wasn't completely healed from the other wounds, so from August to late November, I was out of it again. One more Purple Heart and more agony of the unknown.

I should also say that the doctors removed multiple shrapnel fragments from the left side of my neck, shoulder, chest, trunk, and face. By the start of January 1964, I came down with some terrific malaria and was hospitalized again. The battalion had about two more months of combat duty before we were relieved by new people. So through all the bad weather we had, we were fighting for our lives. In some battles, we were constantly sprayed with Agent Blue and White, and finally Agent Orange. We called it the Vietnam Kangaroo Jock Itch because it was a terrible rash between the legs, as well as other places. I still suffer from it all over my body.

Our encounters with snakes could fill volumes. One of the Cong's favorite booby traps was a hole full of pit vipers. If you stepped into it, you only had about a step and a half to take. We ambushed a lot of would-be ambushers, mostly because we were careful and quiet.

Everything they shot at us was made by the Russians or the Soviet Bloc. They had their AK47, a terrifying weapon to have shot at you. One weakness it had, though, was the distinctive noise it made when the last shot was made, so we knew when they were out of ammo and had to reload. Also, when they snapped off the safety latch we could hear it a block away. We survived by picking up on those things. For another popular booby trap, they would fill a law tube full of grenades with the pins pulled, and as soon as you hit the trip wire the grenades would spill out. This was called "getting your shit lit". One time I hit a law tube full of grenades and they spilled out in front of us, but whoever set up the booby trap forgot to pull the pins out of them first, and they never went off. Talk about lucky sons of bitches.

That was us sometimes and other times everything went wrong and whole units went down the drain. If you didn't watch where you stepped, you could hit a trip wire around the neck.

Charlie was always elusive unless he outnumbered us. Sometimes we left our Prick 25 radios on, and Charlie would come to investigate the radio and we'd either call in arty, or ambush them ourselves. One day we got real lucky, and our point man saw some NVA, North Viet regulars just laying in the grass talking. We were so close, we could hear them talking and smell the cigarettes on their breath. They just came over the DMZ, and acted like they had the world by the ass. We scouted them out and estimated around 40 to 50. This was considered a large group to ambush and would have to be done right. We were on a location later named Camp Carroll. There were about ten of us on a recon patrol when we spotted them. The rule of thumb when setting up a killing ambush is to make sure they're all alone, so you don't get overrun by a large force that may be coming to meet them somewhere close by.

After making sure they were alone, we set up our L-shape ambush along with a minuet ambush down the trail. We put our M-60 at the corner of the L shape and M-14s set up on full fire on their bipods. We put M-79 Bloopers rounds into them first. This got the survivors of the blast to run our way, and we cut them down in about two minutes, every last swinging dick of them. They didn't know what hit them.

We were all delighted in our ambush patrol, but sometimes things were just the other way around. Just before sunset one night, we were dug in around a place called the Rockpile when a large concentration of NVA and VC were set on overrunning us. We fought them all night long and finally we got the air support we needed; the planes came in and dropped Napalm right on them. If it hadn't been for that air cover, we would still be sitting in shit creek.

Talk about creeks and rivers, and you're talking

leeches. They suck your blood and crawl up your ass and infect you. Some Marines would cross a waterway and the leeches would look like Christmas tree tinsel hanging off them. Salt and fire would remove them, and so did aftershave. At night, the cobras would be on the prowl. A lot of troops, VC and American alike, died from deadly encounters with them. At least the snakes killed the enemy too, they didn't discriminate.

We shot a water buffalo by mistake one night, right in the middle of a rice paddy. Sometimes the water and mud in a rice paddy could drown you. We ran across some Australians and Republic of Korea ROKS in our travels. The ROKS really had it in for Charlie. They set up capture patrols and brought them in. Then they usually tortured them to death.

After what seemed like years in 'Nam, we were awarded some R&R (rest and relaxation) in Bangkok, Thailand. Needless to say, we had a ball. Where there's booze and women, do you really need anything else? We returned to the country and what do I do? Step on a punji stake. It was covered with excrement no less, and damn if I didn't get hit in the butt again with a flying piece of metal. It was a"puncture-your-boot-or-leg" boobytrap with a grenade hooked on, to give you the toe popper. Another thing about Vietnam, you never left trash around because the VC picked it up and used it to boobytrap you later. We always buried our c-ration cans or anything else we threw away. If you shit, can it, bury it. We always policed our area well, so they wouldn't know we were there.

I found out Kennedy was killed while I was being treated for shrapnel injuries on my neck and shoulder. At first, I couldn't believe it. We thought they were talking about PFC Kennedy, who was in our platoon of supporting Buttplates at the emergency field hospital in Saigon. Anyway, after catching that toe popper ass backwards, they took out shrapnel fragments from my trunk and face. It was not very enjoyable. Nothing like the man who probes for metal, he can really make you hurt.

We were about four clicks from entering the Ashau Valley that late fall, Valkyrie and Valhalla open its gates for the KIAs missing in action and wounded. I had to shit real bad so I dropped back as the other marines moved on. As they moved on, shit pain hit me and I left my M-14 rifle on the other side of the trail. As I was getting thru, about eight NVA soldiers came down the trail and saw me the same time I saw them. I had my 8 shot 22 H&R revolver in a shoulder holster loaded with 22 long rifle hollow points, I jerked out Roscoe my flat bush issue firearm and hit the deck firing into the group. I dropped about six of them and the other two ran down the trail into the other marines waiting for them. I heard about 40 shots, one grenade would have got them all but I had no grenade with me. Later on we found 14 Special Forces tied upside down by their ankles, they had been apparently caught sleeping and killed after being captured. It looked like the one who was supposed to be on guard fell asleep and the enemies did a job on them. Only one crawled into the undergrowth and died. After they stabbed him we found a note saying "In case of emergency please notify the devil in hell!" Another guy started a letter saying " please don't cry, I am not going to die." All of a sudden a goonie was coming on a bike, we caught him and ate his dried rice and meatballs and he spat at us. He jumped for a rifle and we shot him.

Later on, I heard the 7th Marines had captured 120 Hard Corps (North Viet Regulars). They had L shaped them with 3-M-60's means the machine gun has no friends except the operator behind it. We moved under the cover of darkness and noise. As we were taking two prisoners, a goonie had a AK47 on his back, he leaned forward and the other one behind him started shooting at us, killing three marines before we shot them. And here we are in the valley of death you could always find a fight in here. We were in an old French Bunker feeding the rats as big as a small dog. When we left, we bid them a fond goodbye.

As we entered another bunker, we first ran into contact with the enemy and all I could hear all night long was the beating of pans and they used bull horns to scare us. An NVA Lt. said he was a graduate of Standford University Class of 1959. They out numbered us about 15-1. We heard a loud shouting of threats that if they catch us they will cut our nuts out and make us eat it. The patrol and I were down to not too much ammo and the outcome would be hand to hand time. Our radio was not working and it was still dark so the air people couldn't see us yet. This North Viet Officer kept cursing us in perfect English calling USMC Mad Dogs and not Devil Dogs. When first morning light came he was yelling and cursing the United States and us as he raised up his head above the skyline to holler more shit. I got off a shot at him with the 14 and I saw him lurch over backwards and then silence. Everyone said scratch one Luke as he bought the farm about 0600. They dropped the mortars for a long interval and here they came running to us about 75 to 80 of them running like Joe Shit the Ragman with some white goonies, 9 Russians and Soviet Advisers in front of them leading the way. By that time we had about maybe 150 7.62 MM rounds left in our machinegun. We dropped about 40 of them as all our rounds were linked into 7.62 gun belt. When getting over run and there was no arty or air support or much ammo left, shoot every enemy in sight, make all shots count. Then it's bayonet and entrenching tool time. If you have any mortars or claymores they are a luxury that will buy some time if your radios work and you have flare smoke if, if, if, but we did not have that luxury. As we ducked down, we Fixed Bayonets and hid down low waiting for the first ones to run up on us.

We had remembered the assault training when you only have fixed bayonets, you hide from their bullets till the last second and then scream and ram into them take them by surprise. Startle the oncoming enemy, bayonet him (rifle but) stroke the enemy charge rapidly and run over them, attack and stab them. Take charge kill, go down fighting to the last marine! And we did! A handful of us completely routed about 40 NVA and the Soviet Bloc Advisers who ran at us. They left their rifles, machineguns, grenades and boxes of ammo.

We had been taught this Infantry bayonet method, over and over and over at Camp LeJuene and Camp Pendleton, California thousands of times so we knew instinctively to take charge, kill the man, take over their arms, rifles, machineguns and grenades, everything so we would have a fighting chance. We said "Gung Ho" means Work together double up in twos, back to back and destroy them and we did at a horrible cost in lives to us. We screamed US Marines M-14 Rifle-Bayonet killing machine America's most dreadful secret weapon, a U.S. Marine with the rifle and bayonet. Then around 30 NVAs and 3 white Soviet Advisors who were 1/2 the way up the hill turned around and started to run away. We turned their own machinegun on them, we cut them down like a lawn mower does grass. Gung Ho! We were now down to 5 marines who were able bodied enough to meet the advancing goonies head on as their arty and mortars kept falling. We just kept moving hopefully out of it, not into it (keep alive). I saw the SKS and AK47 bayonets glinting in the sun and the bullets flying by as they shot from the hip while running at us under their own mortar and artillery attack umbrella. When the 3rd and 4th wave started to reach our position, we threw their grenades back to them and fired their rifles and machineguns point blank at their chest and faces out of the corner of my eye. I saw one of our copters being shot down after it crashed and I saw a white face coming our way. We hollered at him to take care because we thought he was a crewman but it was a mistake because he was another white Goonie Advisor coming our way. Two of us dived into a low spot as he fired an AK 47 at us. By this time every one of us seemed to be killed, wounded or gone, and out of my sight I couldn't even hear them anymore and had the feeling of suddenly being abandoned or deserted. I said "Why did all of you die and leave me alone in here?" After the dust cleared I could see clearly and there were about 20 enemies left. They got in with us, the few who were left. I could smell the gook's breathe when he jumped on me.

They tossed about 6 or 7 grenades at us. Before diving into our holes, their dead bodies and ours were piled up all over in stacks of 2 or 3 or more. I heard a ringing in my ears from an explosion near by. But somehow I knew in my heart that they couldn't handle us because we were too well trained. All around us they came the first gook to reach me. I swung my entrenching tool into his face. My E tool had been half masted for smashing bodies it ran thru my mind, hate-evil, unrest disorder and I seemed to be in another place. I felt something sharp caught me in the groin. As I looked around, four of our badly wounded Marines were being bayoneted and clubbed to death. The goonies that were confronting us by then were in a mob. I shot my 45 caliber pistol directly into them, then we were down to only three left when all of a sudden this Soviet was on top of me. He stabbed me in my chest. "Whitey" a marine clubbed him over the head with a rifle and suddenly the gooks ran back retreating from us. Leaving, they were gone and suddenly what was left of our people.. a rose up and those who could not, just lay there, just like the scene in the movie Dantes Inferno I had been stabbed in my chest, groin and fragments in my back and legs. I was walking in a hurt locker, two marines were not hit at all so they attended to our wounded and the dead.

The goonies were stacked up 4 deep in front of our machinegun. You could see where the battle started and where it ended. We found a radio and got on the horn. Help was on the way while marines including myself were bleeding to death. We couldn't do anything about it as we had very little First Aid Equipment. We used goonie First Aid equipment but just about all of our wounded were dead or dying. The First Aid packets from North Vietnam were mailed from Sweden and Berkeley, California.

I was so thirsty and we hadn't any chow for hours, we were looking for another attack that never came. The two unwounded Marines gathered up all the weapons and ammo, and everything they could find, they had to get ready to get hit again. They had 7 prisoners, 6 NVAs, 325 Bravo and one Russian Major called Ivan Shitski. He could talk English to a certain extent. We questioned him and the other NVA s, one DiaUy and the other enlisted men too. We found a letter in his ass pack, from Moscow, USSR. We found out that he was in the 9th Parachute Regt. Russian Airborne. He begged us to kill him as it was a disgrace to be captured. The other 6 NVAs were not talking. They were told that as soon as the copters got there, they would be thrown out of the copter at about four thousand feet, they would soon meet their maker splashing into the ground. The Russian got the same message. Here came the copter, they tied the NVAs hand and foot, put them with the wounded marines being medical evacuated, we told the Russian to watch. Here came the goonies falling out of the sky. We told him he was the next , and they loaded him in the copter. Then we chanted "We're alive! We're alive!"

Sergeant Koski 3rd MARINE DIVISION
in May 1967,
Combat Veteran of two
tours in Vietnam.

41.

The doctors also checked that one bayonet wound I got while tangling with the NVA up north. They found it healed very well. I was glad to hear that, because it penetrated my left lung and exited out my back. That was one episode in my life that I was very glad to have survived—especially considering the odds we were up against: about seven to one.

After the punji stake healed, we pulled a capture detail and took along this Kit Carson (chieu hoi). That's what they called guys who defected from a VC BN. He said he was born up in the Cam Lo area and could help us as a guide. As soon as we made a prisoner snatch, we were crossing some gullies on the Laos border. We ran into some gooks, camped out right in front of our chopper pick-up area. The chieu hoi fired his gun off to warn them, we shot him and made for the incoming bird. The lead was flying thick and fast, and the chopper took a direct B-40 hit and went down in flames. There went our ride, too, so we shot the other Vietnamese we captured and made our fast tracks out of there. About 200 NVA chased us, so we set up grenade trip wires in a few places where they would be running through in hot pursuit after us.

We got some of them, but needed air support bad. We were shooting it out, near the end of our ropes, when here comes those beautiful jets. They dropped napalm and other high explosives right on them. When napalm hits close it sucks your breath away, and you're covered in waves of heat. They came back and strafed the gooks, too. The dinks had a 51-cal mounted on a truck and they made it real hot for those flyers. A few ran off in our direction and we popped them head on. Real soon here comes a UH34 Delta bird who located us by flare smoke, otherwise it would have been a long, dangerous walk back. After that grenade went off near my right ear, I never could hear that good again. After all these narrow escapes, according to the law of averages, you'd think my time was running out fast. Lord knows, that thought was in my mind a lot.

Whenever we were near any of the local bars, in Da nang, Quang Tri, Conthien, Chu Lai or wherever, I got a little beer and broad time. I got to know a lot of females while there, and in a lot of different parts of Eye Corps, two Corps, plus when down at Saigon, Vung Tau, and Tan An.

As long as you had the Jing Wa, piaster or green stuff, you were doing ok. When living in hooches you never got used to it, and whenever on search and destroy missions, they used to hang poisonous snakes in their doorways. The most popular one was a Krate; it bit you in the face and neck because you couldn't see it in time.

We spent what seemed like an eternity in the fields, and we suffered a hell of a lot of casualties, mostly from those damn boobytraps that blew your leg off. By late January, it was time to Di Di Mau dinky Dau or rotate. Too many monsoons, too much red clay, too much ever present dust and terrible heat. Too much death and destruction.

One day when we were down to about a month, we were on a fire base outpost near Khe Sanh, reinforced with teak wood in our bunker and sandbagged like a good mother. All of a sudden we had sappers feeling us out, and we got hit by mortars. I guess they were giving us a good-bye present. After fighting them off all night, and calling in an air strike to run them off, we found out three of the VC sappers were women and they had babies on their backs. We had been so close to them, the enemy was hanging all over our concertina wire. We used up all the Claymore mines we had, and just about everything else. When we took over this old French used fire base, we found some ten or so skeletons. They looked like our guys, but no dog tags. They were buried in a wall of the bunker. A direct hit unearthed them from the wall, the graves' people bagged them up and disposed of them. There were several M-2 carbines, and we found some Springfield 1903 rifles with them. When they were medivacing our dead and wounded out, it took the choppers four trips in and out. When we checked out the enemy dead, we found about six Caucasian looking bodies. One, I am sure, and possibly two, were French. They were no doubt helping Charlie, so he'd leave their rubber plantations alone. The other four had Russian and East German identifications on them. They were no doubt advisors for the Goonies.

The night before, we saw in our parachute flares a Caucasian looking individual. He appeared to have a long scar across his entire left eye and cheek. I shot at him, but somehow I missed him. He had been very bold, and while throwing grenades, he was swearing at us. He looked like a DiaUy, a captain in the NVA. That night always stayed with me, and one night in San Francisco, around 1984, I was on a bus going somewhere down Van Ness Ave, I think. That asshole stepped on the bus, and I recognized him the same time he recognized me. There was that scar, no mistake about it. He knew I remembered him, because he jumped off the bus and took off running. No doubt he was mixed Caucasian and probably North Vietnamese. Once you saw him, you could never forget his scar or manner or looks.

When we were in the country, the goonies put a price on our heads, dead or alive, because we assisted the South Vietnamese: taught them how to fight and use our weapons. We lost a lot of good people because of that bounty. The bad part was you couldn't tell a South Vietnamese from a VC, and if you were by yourself with them at night, you could kiss your ass goodbye. They would take off their outside clothes, and all you would see were their black pajamas. They loved to stick a knife in your back, but there were hundreds of ways they'd kill you. Even at this early stage in the war, there was a feeling of distrust. Not being able to communicate with them didn't exactly help matters. We all did our best to train them, under those terrible circumstances. It was like having your arm tied behind your back, no doubt.

There were thousands of patriotic Vietnamese out there. They paid the price for being our allies. To be honest, I could only think of one thing: we only had a week to go. We were real short timers. When sappers blew up the White Elephant in Da Nang, I was back in the head sitting, straddling a slit trench. I couldn't have been in a better place at the time of explosion. I was so drunk I didn't even know what happened. The place was in shambles, people dying or dead all over. Half of the place was just plain gone. I mean, you could see Danang City out the back hole. Sabotage was getting more regular. Just a week before, a kid walked into a bunch of tankers and blew everything up. He had a tank mine on him, and was selling soda, we found out later. You didn't drink any of that from them, because it had ground glass mixed in. What a bunch of fanatics!

The last run-in we had with a VC and NVA outfit, we had to call in more air and naval fire. This was on the DMZ at Conthien. We were getting really short; a few others and I were down to a week or so. We were showing some ARVN soldiers how to set themselves in for all night when we started to get hit with cluster fuck stuff, and Russian Propelled Grenades, or RPG's. I couldn't believe things could go so wrong so quick. They had white phosphorous, or Wooley Peter, hitting our area. The AVRN went wild and ran and we were all alone, so we called in arty to fire for effect. They had to hit directly on us, because by this time the enemy was right in with us. We were firing point blank at each other and told arty to rake the four sides. They were perfect, we got a hold of air and they napalmed the hordes that were running our way. In the dying rays of the sunlight, you could see crispy critters everywhere. Where an army was running toward us, now there were just black, burnt out figures. Still, it was hand to hand in the dusk. I ran into our bunker to reload my M-14 when three figures darkened the hatchway. I loaded just fast enough to get a magazine in my rifle. I shot them, and here come five more but someone shot them from behind. For about an hour I was beginning to think they would never stop coming. We were finally down to a dozen healthy Marines. The gooks had three ladders thrown over the wire fence; there were bodies everywhere, ours and theirs. Our first lieutenant went down with four dead gooks on him. After grenading their bodies outside the fire base, we hung on until morning. During the night they came back to get their dead and we claymored and shot more of them.

For the most part, we were just hoping we wouldn't get hit again before dawn. We were finally getting relieved by fresh troops. They put all our dead guys on the cargo net, the chopper flew straight up and over us, and we were sprayed and showered with the blood of the corpses, a final salute from our once living Marines The next bird to land wasn't so lucky. It landed on a 105 boobytrap hidden under the corrugated steel landing pad, and just evaporated. The chopper's runner must have come in contact with the firing pin on the 105 Howitzer round.

On our flight down from the Conthien area, we took some very heavy fire from enemy 51-caliber machine guns. We had to force land almost upside down. One thing for sure, I grabbed on to all I could get a hold of, including Wingchi, a Marine falling out the door. I got a hold of his ass pack, and between the two of us, we rode it down inside. We were in serious trouble again, air support was flying in to strafe the patrols sent to kill us.

One thing to remember in battle, maybe the most important thing, was never return the way you came. You're just asking to be ambushed. Thank our lucky stars for some alert air cover and a good radio still working! There were a lot of walking wounded and supine wounded all leaving the same day I did. Our tour was over and we were still alive. Maybe not well, but alive. No more tunnels to crawl in and duck the hanging snake, no more patrols, no more getting overrun by superior numbers, no more rocket attacks, or ground fire, no more booby trap trip wires, or snake pits, or monsoons, or heat. No more leeches, no more going days without a wink of sleep. When we did sleep, we built a fire to fool the gooks and then crashed in some thick underbrush, leaving one man awake for security.

Chapter 5

I was up for Corporal E-4, and "Okinawa, here I come!" for a medical checkup. The last time I saw Vietnam as a grunt was over a wing tip on a C-130 leaving Tan Son Nhut air base in February 1964. I got orders from the Rock to report to Quantico, Virginia. First I had 30 days to get there, by military HOPS, but I was still hurting in my rectal area from that shrapnel in my buttocks and groin area. I also had some problems with that RPG concussion, but I didn't elaborate to the doctors on it. When it happened, I was blacked out for a long time.

After pulling 30 days, or 28 of them, I was reporting into E and I Company at Camp Barret, Virginia. I had just flown in from San Francisco, California, and what a change in the weather! It was 50 when I left San Francisco, and about 30 at Camp Barrett in Virginia. In Enlisted Instructor Company area, I caught a bad cold and had bad chest pains. Then I came down with pneumonia again, so had three days' bed rest on fluids at Quantico Naval Hospital. This probably came on as a result of the most vigorous exercise with some 100-pound sandbags that we were lifting when I first reported in.

I made corporal and was a decorated Marine, so I had a lot of pull around there. Our job was to teach would-be second lieutenants how to fire the M-60 machine gun. One day the student louies from the basic school were firing away. All of a sudden, four of them ran out towards their targets for no apparent reason and the hot barrel on the gun made it cook off, firing by itself. All four were killed instantly. All four or five of the range personnel were transferred, and the accident was written off as quietly as possible.

Meanwhile, I put in for Marine Corps physical fitness school at Henderson Hall in Arlington, VA. It took eight weeks to finish, and was a good hard course with a lot of running, swimming, rope climbing, and push-ups. At or

47.

around Arlington National Cemetery, we also did a lot of weight lifting. I came out first in our class of 75 people. At night after training, I visited my Uncle Mike who lived nearby. Those were good times.

I returned to TBS (The Basic School) at Quantico and began teaching body building and endurance to the junior and senior officers. My job was very prestigious. I was working in the company of officers and teaching them how to lift weights correctly. What a racket!

My good friend Frenchy was driving his TR3 with my good friend Jeep and me, when he overturned astraddle of a ditch. If it wasn't for the ditch we all would have been killed. The way it was, that ditch saved our lives, keeping us from being crushed to death. The cockpit of the car was open, and right below us the deep ditch kept our heads from hitting the ground, and the car from crushing us. Jeep still suffered a broken right wrist. There were so many auto accidents—everyone trying to get there the last second from their liberties. Then they go and end up having a car accident, maybe getting killed. It seemed like every day we heard some Marines were getting killed in auto accidents en route to Camp Barrett. We could have all ended up on the death list that day. The car was still drivable, at least it didn't catch fire before it was upright.

Jeep and Frenchy were with me on our first tour overseas. There were only them and I, plus a few others—the few original survivors from our platoon in boot camp. Jeep was from Baltimore, and we used to sleep off drinks at his house, then we enjoyed a great breakfast, dated some girls and listened to Beatles' music. They were real popular at that time. Frenchy made it through our first tour of Vietnam, but his luck ran out on the second tour. I heard his squad stepped on a mine in a rice paddy.

The rifle range was coming up the next day. There's an old USMC saying: if you miss the enemy at 500 yards, you'll soon be fighting him at five feet with your bayonet. Well, we all fell out for qualification detail. It was late April or early May 1964, and it rained and snowed every day. We all ended up shooting UNK unqualified, this was my first time ever firing a UNK. The stormy weather we had everyday made it impossible even to see the targets, let alone score bull's-eyes. The next detail they sent out in the next two weeks had it made. Their weather was sunny with no wind. We all stood in a formation in front of a Captain Duncle Berger, our CO. He and the first sergeant really lit into us. If they had been out there in the rain and mud with us, they would have known why hardly anyone even shot marksman, but of course they weren't.

We were training second lieutenants—or they would be second louie's if they graduated from the basic school. As fast as possible, I got out of teaching M-60 machine guns to recruit officers, because my title now was Fitness Instructor, which took up all my time. I always ran about five miles after hours, and I did push-ups, sit-ups, deep knee bends, a lot of weight lifting and a lot of swimming in the base pool. I had to keep one step ahead of my students. Some of these cats were just off the football, baseball, track, or swimming teams from various colleges around the country, so they were in incredible shape.

During the summer of 1964, I was never in better shape, despite my wounds from Vietnam. I was running about ten miles a day, and the rest of the time on the obstacle course, gym, or in the pool. I was body training 75 percent of the time. We trained USMC second louie's and the FBI. I trained some agents when I was on the M-60 range, and I also put 4 classes of them through our fitness courses. Between FBI recruits and second lieutenant recruits, I was very busy. I also had a cadre that helped me. There were six of them, all graduated from the fitness school in Arlington, Virginia. We took turns on our times of duty, a "made-in-the-shade" duty. During liberty hours, I went to Richmond, Virginia. I met a girl there named Donna and I spent a lot of time with her. Then one day her brother called and told me she drowned. I was shocked. I didn't even go to the funeral.

49.

One day in the summer or early fall of 1964, I read a bulletin board message looking for force recon Marines. It said that anyone interested should see their chain of command to inquire about the USMC's most elite force." Well, I just came back from Quantico Naval Hospital because of blood from an anal scar, caused by a shell fragment in Vietnam. While I was there, they gave me some lotion for the Vietnam kangaroo jock itch. For the anal area they issued me some suppositories, I also had some arm nerve problems, along with this fungus in the groin and skin splints.

The agent blue and white defoliants were a real rash maker. You always got it around your nuts, because of the jock straps, plus anywhere your clothes were tight. When we first noticed the rashes, we wouldn't figure where they came from.

Everybody in the barracks said I was crazy to join the Force. "Recon Marines get killed," they cried, and just thinking about joining them was nuts. They also said anyone who tries to pass the PT test fails. All I heard was negative things about going. Even my best friends said I should kiss my ass away if I set foot in the back of the Camp Geiger tiger training area.

Down by the coal pile, this is where Second Force Recon's area was, at the east end of second ITRS base at Geiger where we had all gone to train, right from Parris Island, and we left there for three weeks' recruit leave, then returned and left for Camp Pendleton. It would be almost a full circle, and I was in the best shape I have every been in since joining the USMC. "Why not give it a try? The worst that can happen is that I don't make it." I thought it over and figured I was the world's biggest fool. Give up all this plush, easy job for the unknown. We heard about Force Recon from boot camp. Two of our guys from Camp Margarita went and made it, but they were two of the very few. I talked to them after they returned from Fort Benning, Georgia, at Jump School, and they were both very cocky, always daring us to join and take the PT test.

I finally made up my mind: I would try it. In the next few days, I followed the chain of command, and there was no turning back now. The EXO cut orders on me for FMF force troops Lant, Camp Geiger, North Carolina. His parting words were: "So, you want to be a super grunt, huh? Leave this paradise for that? Get the fuck out of my office." I said my goodbyes and all wished me well, and I left in a 1961 white Pontiac Ventura. I called it the Big White Horse, and even had the name painted on the right front fender. My order said I had three days to get there, so I stopped off first in Richmond and had a party with some girls and friends I knew. At long last, I reached Jacksonville.

Camp Geiger was named after General Roy Geiger of World War II fame (his story was made into a movie, *The Great Escape*). As I drove into the Force troops area, I saw people with no hair, and green t-shirts, green swim trunks, and coral shoes running around the area.

There was a skull-and-crossbone flag flying over the company office's hatchway. I parked the car and walked in. I was met head on by the CO, 1st Sergeant Billy Dare. He had a set of pull-up bars over his hatch, and a green parachute draped around his windows. He said: "give me those orders, and get up on that pull-up bar, and don't stop until I say so." He read the orders about six times. I was up to about 45 pull-ups and he said, "You want to be one of us, huh?" He was a big man about 6'5" tall and built like a wrestler. By this time I was really vibrating and he said, "Recover." I dropped back to attention, another force trooper came running in and ordered me at the dead run to put on my sweat gear. I went into my seabag and I was ready in about two minutes. We ran to the pull-up bars, after as many pull-ups as I could get out, I dropped for push-ups, then squat thrusts, and sit-ups, deep knee bends, and all the time being hollered at. It was terrible hot, with no breeze. After what seemed like an hour of this, my legs felt all wobbly and I thought I was blacking out, then we hit the blacktop road for a timed run!

I don't remember finishing, just waking up in a shower stall in the middle of the deck, by the drain. I heard someone shout into the rear of the truck I had arrived at the base swimming pool. Two Force Recon Marines were there to meet me, they threw a scuba mask in the deep end, about 20 feet of water and said, "Dive, put it on and clear it of water as you surface." I passed this test, and then they ordered me to dive in the deep end again, and stay down as long as they did. I was always a good swimmer, but that day I was moving a heavy weight on the bottom of the pool. I almost failed. I thought I was drowning. The last second we secured, and I was never so happy to come out of water. I was cold, tired and ready to fall over. When we got outside, there wasn't a truck, and we ran the three miles back to the Force Recon company area. We cut through the woods, and across a field and a highway. When we reached there, I was met by two snarling fist fights in as many minutes until someone pulled us apart.

In the squad bay, the living area was like every USMC squad bay. I got a rack, a locker box, and a wall locker. No one talked to me at this point. After a while, I got to talking with a guy named PFC Young. He was a big 6'6" guy from Canada. He got me some blankets and sheets, and told me what I could expect in the following days. At least I was among them: the fearless ones. At 1700, liberty call was sounded and I started putting my gear away. The next day at 0530 hours, I was issued my swim trunks, green t-shirts, coral shoes, k-bar-swim flares, green socks, grease gun and ammo.

After all my gear was secured, the CO gunnery sergeant Gunny Rawder said, "Here's your parachute." I ran everywhere with the chute on my back, from morning formation at 0700 until 1630. In the meantime, I practiced PLF (Parachute Landing Falls). I jumped off sideways for side PLF's, I jumped from the box for front side PLF's. This was my four hell weeks, to prepare for jump school at Fort Benning, Georgia. After a while, this can get mighty taxing, and when I was in the chow hall,

all the ITR training Marines would say, "There is one of those Recon Marines," and stare at me in awe!

Well, the four hell weeks passed pretty fast. All I was doing was the same thing I had done the first day, over and over plus everybody in Recon runs everywhere he goes, even officers—CO, EXO, staff, everyone. We were told one day that we were head and shoulders above the average Marine. They cut orders on me for Fort Benning jump school. After all the PT we had been doing at Camp Geiger, North Carolina, including running up and down the coal pile, I was in top shape and ready for anything Fort Benning could throw at me.

One air delivery Marine and I got orders together, so we flew down from Cherry Point, North Carolina, Air Facility. When we arrived at the Fort Benning Airborne check-in area, we were assigned out racks and went to chow. There was a large group of Air Force, Air Sea Rescue, and some Navy Seals, as well as hundreds of Army people.

The next morning, I fell out with some airborne jump boots I had bought in Jacksonville a few days after I started pre-jump school at Camp Geiger, so they were pretty well broken into after a month of PLF's, and obstacle courses and God only knows how much other PT I did getting ready for Fort Benning, Georgia. We fell out of the barracks, and got in what would be our steady places in ranks. We were called to attention, did a left face and a double-time to a large building, and saw a large cadre of airborne instructors.

We were told by a colonel that if we wanted to, we could drop out now and return to our billet areas, and no one would think any less of us. Maybe 10 or 15 guys who were air guard reserves personnel left out the big door. The rest of us stood at parade rest, and then attention when the Colonel left. We were then double-timed, or what they call the "airborne shuffle." We were just starting the first week, called ground week, a replay of my four hell weeks at Camp Geiger. Airborne shuffle everywhere, push-ups, sit-ups, pull-ups, wind sprints.

Some uniform inspections, starched creases on arms and legs, highly polished jump boots, shined brass. We were always called Navy deck apes, or jar Marine heads, or Air Force prop heads by the Airborne cadre.

This was summer, 1965, and talk about hot and humid! When they ordered you to stop an exercise, they would bark out "Recover!" and you would come to the parade rest, but if they sometimes said "Seat cover!" you were back down doing push-ups, or "pushing away Georgia," as we called it. This PT went on with the running distances getting longer everyday. Well, I was doing the physical training fine, because I had been prepared for it ahead of time. A lot of people quit every day, the ranks grew thinner, we started ground week at 0400 every morning, and we secured at 1930 every night. Then we prepared for the morning inspection. Our billets were of World War II vintage.

Friday finally got there, and we finished ground week. Saturday and Sunday we got our uniforms ready for Monday, and rested up. We were warned not to leave the training area, but some guys did anyway. The first sergeant told me: "No Marine's ever failed to graduate at Fort Benning, so don't be the first."

Monday morning, first day of tower week, the start of the second week of training. It was much like the first, except maybe they doubled the PT. We were practicing the parachute landing fall. On the swing land trainer, the SLT as it was called, was a seat oscillating effect and you would jump out of it at heights of 6 to 20 feet into a sawdust or sand pile, by a rope pulled by another man. It was like coming down a clothesline cable and being released. This taught you to make contact with the balls of the feet, the outer leg muscles, the thighs, the push-up muscles and shoulders—the five points of contact. Once we started the 32-foot tower out the door, you could shuffle out a mock door and fall 32 feet on the ground. Doing a PLF (Parachute Landing Fall) they had a parachute harness on us and it was really tight around the family jewels to avoid the jerk from the fall.

We finally jumped the 250-foot tower, and the instructors were not calling us "legs" as much. "Straight legs" is a term for non-jumpers. Well, we passed the weekend again, and Monday we started getting ready to jump out of a C-130's side doors. Monday morning rolled around, third jump week, and we found ourselves inspecting the next man's parachute. Mostly the instructors gave the final ok that all hands were suited up and ready to get into the aircraft to take off. When the green light went on we were standing up, hooking ourselves up to the anchor cable, and all I saw after we had equipment check was a C-130 flying away from me. I was airborne and floating down to the waiting drop zone below. We had four more jumps, one every day that week. If they saw you limping, you could be ordered into the next class, meaning you might not graduate.

That Friday afternoon I finished, and I was proud as a peacock to get those blood wings (novice wings). Wow! I was no longer a straight leg. I was a five-jump airborne trooper. That afternoon we got a guided tour around the Airborne Memorial at Benning, and that night we went to the closest town, and had a whopper of a time, mostly congratulating ourselves on our latest accomplishment. By Monday afternoon, I checked back in with the Force Recon Company DNCO and the people there saw me in a little different light. "Well," Captain Sheridan said, "you need five more jumps to get your gold wings." So on the next weekend, he flew a UH-34 Delta out of New River Air Facility and we completed five more jumps on a Sunday afternoon.

I had a girlfriend named Margarita standing on the ground watching the whole thing. Captain Sheridan assigned three men from our CO squad to help. Then we all went to Jayville, North Carolina, and from there to Virginia, flying all the way. I dropped Margarita off at the Greyhound bus depot at Oceana, Virginia, and she left for Washington D.C.. The rest of the company arrived there one day later. We were to be jumping in an air show. We were billeted at the Navy base there. We had some good fist fights with the sailors at their bar, because they resented us being there. Funny, no one really liked Recon. Was it jealousy? Were they afraid of us, or maybe we were just cocky? Maybe it was a combination. I'll never know.

Our slogan was: "A snake, in the grass, a fish in the water, a bird in the air. Some here, some there, and some everywhere." We were always being loaned out to the leg companies as the aggressors. Every day I was in the CO area, we ran ten miles and swam another ten. There used to be miles of tar-paper covered pipes with asphalt inter-layered to protect the pipes from freezing in the winter. They were all over Camp Geiger, about 30 feet in the air. Sometimes we would walk these pipes, and the second ITR recruits would say, "There goes a Force Recon." They were in awe of us, and probably down deep in the heart of every red blooded Marine, they all wondered if they should try out for our PT test.

We did get 2 radio MOS boot 2nd ITR Marines after testing 500 people; our sergeants who were testing people chose 2. The biggest I ever saw the company was 95, and 1st Force Recon at Delmar, California, had only about 80—175 out of the whole 300,000 in the Corps, trying to make a point. When officers took our PT test, they got the same treatment as enlisted. No breaks for anyone. It seemed like we couldn't get a soul to qualify, better to have the best than most.

Just about every night we had a jump with full equipment, meaning rifle, long general purpose bag or short general purpose bag (GPB) as they were called. We carried the radio, ammo, parts, food, sleeping bags, you name it. Well, we had been all over the country as aggressors, so I had about 25 jumps by this time under my belt. This particular night, six of us were jumping the famed C-1 Alpha. Captain Carroll was our jump master. He was killed in Vietnam later by a navy short round shell. They named Camp Carroll after him. Anyway, the doors or hatches on this type of fixed-wing aircraft are only about 4.5 feet high, so when I jumped, I just somersaulted out head first. I also had a long GPB hooked to my harness D rings. I looked up and no canopy.

Falling like a rock, I pulled my reserve chute out and it simply wraps around my unopened main chute. "Oh, shit," I said, "I'm screwed now." As I plunged down in the dark of night, I was passing by all these open chutes, and kept going.

Luckily, I landed in some trees and they broke my fall. God bless those trees. Sergeant Campbell was the first on the scene. When he found out I was still alive, he said it was a miracle. The worst injury was a bruise on my foot. I was on crutches for awhile, but luckily, I could still walk. I found out later that I fell 1,200 feet.

Well, the next morning I fell out for inspection with my gold wings on upside down, to signify the jumper went all the way in without either chute opening. In 1962, in that same drop zone, one of our former COs died. He was free falling and just creamed into a field. He was Captain Jo Hansen, USMC. We also had one of our 1st lieutenant's reserve chute pop open in a COG-12. He was pulled out the door and his neck broke. He was dead by the time he floated to the ground.

Trunk Operators and Submarine Operators (OPS) Recon trained all of its people to be trunk operators. This meant that the trunk operator of the operation was the first into the trunk of the moving sub. He would be responsible for getting the first swimmer inside the trunk and adjusting the water pressure inside the sub. After diving about 40 feet to get in, all recon swimmers were, to put it lightly, somewhat out of air. Sometimes they would let loose a floater, a colored orange balloon. We would see it and go down the rope. That was the easy way to find the trunk, but somewhat slower in descent. The other way was after swimming two miles out and straddling and floating and treading water and waiting.

The sub came and we dove for the sub trunk door. If we were really lucky, we might be able to transport by light rubber craft and wait for the sub. As it approached near us, we would dive for it. Then the other recon who was manning the (LRC) light rubber craft would head for shore. Once in the sub trunk, the trunk ops would force the water out of the trunk, and we would enter the watertight compartment and enter the sub.

It was always cold and clammy inside the outer watertight compartments. Once inside the main sub, the Navy would look at us like we were underwater creatures, but we always got along pretty well with them. Force Recon Marines, Special Forces and Navy Seals were the only people to enter underwater through their sub trunks.

After getting to our destination, whether it was off the coast of South America or the Virgin Islands, we would make our ascent out the trunk, and upward to the surface. There we would swim in and do our hydro-recon on the beach for sentries. It was our job in time of war to do these things for real. If it was a wartime mission, we killed the sentries and planted explosives on the enemy's doorstep. In Cuba for instance, we landed there four times undetected.

On the Sub Ops we mainly worked out of St. Croix, St. Thomas, all the main Virgin Islands. The water there is the clearest in the world. We worked with Seal Team 11 on two different missions. When we pulled liberty in the same bar together, it was the custom for every man to spit a green saliva into the beer pitcher being passed around and the last man at the table drank the entire contents and so on until every man drank in his turn. We had a lot of trouble keeping the peace, with two outfits like this under the same roof. No love was ever lost. I just returned to Camp Geiger and I had orders for scuba school at Key West, Florida. Well we, one other Force guy and me, took one week of pre-scuba training in the base pool and flew to Key West by C-130 express. When you arrived, you saw a large welcome sign saying, "You are now entering the breathing apparatus school, only the best make it into the best." Anyway, we were taught all the gas mixture formulas, and buddy breathing by taking turns when there is only one source of air from one set of air tanks, and one regulator.

This was a month of a lot of PT and deep water swimming. Key West, the "city of sin," was off limits to training personnel, but Jim, this guy I knew, and I visited the famous Key West. The bars were wild, and the SPs, MPs and police were everywhere.

Chapter 6

Well, we graduated from scuba school and I received my scuba head insignia. Now I was airborne-scuba trained. As soon as I got back, I started jump master classes. This qualified me to jump people out of an aircraft door into certain jump zones. I also got my jump master blaster wings, we were going to Jacksonville, North Carolina, every chance we had. When all we had was base area liberty, we had two bars that were our own. One was called Chad's and Martha's, and the other was the Double Eagle. These were exclusive Force Recon bars.

I met a girl named Rita in Washington D.C., and we went together for a few months. She had a chance to meet our whole company, and I guess she wasn't too impressed. Anyway, I spent a lot of time with her, but her father didn't like me too well. I bought her a ring and she kept the ring, but told me the engagement was off. I went to her apartment and had a brawl with her father and brother. I never did get my ring back, although I put them away on the deck. They called the D.C. Police Department, but the family never pressed any charges against me. I never saw Rita again. I saw her sister, and she told me she got married, so I said to hell with it.

I got orders for ranger school at Fort Benning, Georgia, so away I went. Eight weeks and a day of training at Dahlonega, Georgia, Elgin Air Force Base, Florida, and all over Benning. Map and compass land navigation. Check points to make at a certain time, no sleep, plenty of endurance. Everybody said if they can make it we can, too. It was almost like Camp Pendleton all over. We ate rattlesnake, drank helezoned water, ran through obstacles at night that would have been thought to be impossible during the day. We learned all the fine arts of sneak and poop. Honed our skills in the bush to a fine perfection. When I graduated from Fort Benning, Georgia, as a Ranger Special Forces trained, I earned the Green Beret.

Ranger school is physically and mentally demanding, as is U.S. Marine Infantry training. The two are both very tough to get through, one as tough as the other.

Our mastery of this Ranger training came from intense patrolling with Force Recon and from another time in Vietnam. We had learned all the basics at Camp Pendleton and other places like Korea, Borneo, PI, Okinawa, Japan, and Guadalcanal. So putting it all together, I just didn't come off the street and go into Ranger School. The day I graduated, I got to sew my Ranger patch on my recon swim trunks; that was one of my proudest days. Now I was a Force Recon, airborne, jump master, Scuba Special Forces Ranger.

They didn't waste any time sending us to the pickle meadows in Bridgeport, California. First, we flew to Fallon, Nevada, and started our Sere School Training. When we got there, it was cold. We had a three-week course on more good old bush training; survival, escape, resist, and evade. At Fallon, an Air Force officer accidentally got his eye shot out with a blank fired in his face. This happened when the aggressors charged into the classroom (Quonset hut) and attempted to take everyone prisoner. I and several more escaped. There were five of us, all Recon Force, that they never caught. The aggressors were from 1st Force Recon, so we had some very able people after us. If they caught you, you were locked into cages, and treated just like POWs. I heard some horror stories about the people who were caught. They were beat up and not fed food or water.

The five of us were lucky we had fled Cherry Point, North Carolina. The reason we escaped together was we were all right next to each other and jumped out a window in the confusion and blended into the countryside. We had no coats, no food, no nothing. We boiled wild onions and made soup in our canteen cups.

The only way to keep warm was to keep moving. The aggressors almost caught us two different times, but we hid from them. Finally, when the problem was secured after two weeks, we could return. The five of us still brag

61.

about not being caught. Recons work swift, silent, and deadly. The area that we had been avoiding getting caught in was some of the roughest terrain I had ever been in, between Western Nevada and the Southeastern Sierras of California.

Anyhow, we flew back to good old Cherry Point, North Carolina, and had successfully completed escape and survival school. All I had to eat those weeks of survival was rabbits we snared, some birds and snakes, and onion soup made from wild onions, so I lost a few pounds. We also practiced some of our summer mountain leader training by repelling off of some dead end places, like cliffs and steep canyon walls, when we had been evading the aggressors. It's nice to know that we had our repelling gear with us among other things that really came in handy.

Meanwhile, in between this hectic training, I had a spur removed from my left heel. Some light duty, and I was back to the old grind. I had this done at the Camp Pendleton Hospital in California after we had orders for Camp Pendleton from Camp Le Jeune, North Carolina when they took off the spur called Chronic Planter Fascitis off my left heel. They dissolved it by injection of the medication (cortizone) in the right foot. This was resulting from the injuries sustained by that 1,250-foot fall I had taken at Mile Hamock Bay drop zone. I was lucky no spur had to be removed from my right foot, also.

Before we had left Camp Le Jeune, we were living at Onslow Beach. There, our Marine and Naval engineers had constructed a near perfect replica of the Hanoi Hilton and surrounding area.This was top secret and only a few of us know about it. The first sergeant back at Camp Geiger had called a CO's formation, and we knew something was up. I had just returned from New London, Connecticut, for sub training and just about everyone who wasn't away at jump school, ranger school, scuba school or somewhere else was there in the formation.

For security reasons, we had been told to fall into the area between the scuba locker, where we kept our air and gear for scuba tanks, and the parachute loft where chutes were dried out, tree limbs removed, holes sewn up, and all kinds of things done to the material so it would be serviceable to jump again—like completely hanging the whole canopy up on special hooks to dry it out with special air temps in the parachute loft.

The parachute riggers had a good life mending, sewing, washing, and drying out T-10 parachutes of olive drab color. Anyway, some of these chutes had to be chopped out of trees that they were ensnared in. These chopped-topped trees were really dangerous for unwitting jumpers who could possibly be impaled. That's why we all wore tailbone sponges to safeguard against impalement or any other rectal injuries or, at least, hopefully.

Well, when I had been up to Fort Lee, Virginia, at parachute riggers' school, we had heard something was in the air, and now most of us were standing in a circle wondering what's up. We had also had two or three ARVN Vietnamese advisors, they called themselves. They were all Di auy (captains). There was something going on that would mess up our good Recon routine. We had all marched into the riggers loft by now.

Every Force Recon Marine there was beating his brains out to figure why the hell this formation. The Major got down to brass tacks fast, he said, "You all know about the Hilton mock build-up in back of Onslow Beach?" Some of us were aware of it. "Yes! Well you all know this is top secret and classified." We were not aware of that, but we were listening. The building had guards at all the doors so no one could hear outside and the windows were all shut. "Well men, we need some volunteers. I would like it if we can only get single men, with at least 2 years left on your enlistments. We are going to need about 40 men for this work, but we will be training around 60 in case anyone needs to be replaced for one reason or another. Now I know the majority of you are

63.

triple threats—airborne, scuba, and ranger trained. You have been around this Force Recon work a lot so, you are considered qualified for what lays ahead." Again, I said to myself, *what lays ahead.* "You who are picked will be briefed in more depth later. All I can say is this will be no piece of cake, and from this point on is confidential. By the way, 1st Force Recon is also working on this project as we stand here. As you know there, is a war going on in Vietnam. We are forming a 5th Force Recon also to help reinforce 3rd Force Recon. Well, good luck, good training, God speed. You are going to need it."

So, as we exited, we were all called to attention. The first sergeant then found out through the CO office who was going to ship over or extend, who was married, and who was getting out or going on different orders somewhere else that precluded this. With this settled, I was selected and just about all the single guys, and three married men volunteered. So we ate, breathed, slept, and lived the Hanoi Hilton. We trained with blanks and live ammo, but first we would get a briefing on the day's events, reminding us no talking on liberty or to parents, lovers, friends, relatives, no one! We were told only the CIA was aware of it, and I didn't know any CIA. For weeks we jumped in at 0400 in the morning, a lot of times going in the waterways, or the ocean around Onslow Beach, but after a while we started hitting the drop zone. It was a matter of slipping correctly and pulling down a part of the canopy so you would drop almost directly on the mark. Going into the waterways or ocean could be dangerous in the dark because of the swift current or the possibility of hitting into the surf line with all the strong undertow. We were all well trained in exiting out of a blowing canopy over your head while hitting the water. One could drown if the canopy or harness pulled you under.

Soon, we prided ourselves on not getting wet. We always had 3 or 4 UH-34 Delta Copters at our disposal. Every 0330, we loaded up at New River Air Facility, North Carolina. Soon we knew every pilot there. If you wanted to sleep, you'd better hit the rack at 1800 (6:00 p.m.), or by Friday you would be sleepwalking. We were told 1st Force at Del Mar, California, and 5th Force and 3rd Force were on the same training we were in Okinawa. So misery loves company. We weren't alone after we became proficient enough to hit every time we jumped low level (no reserve). So, if something went wrong, like a Mae West malfunction to bad sucker, you were warned. Your mother told you that parachuting was a way not to get old and gray, or she should have.

While we were covering this first phase of entry training, we were also covering some other aspects at the same time—identifying certain landmarks and terrain features. We had learned from F-104 pilot reports by flying low level just outside Hanoi City that we would see the Karst Hills, and at almost the same time we would spot the area north of Than Hoa, called armpit south of the inlet Nam Din. As we raced over these areas, the paper bridge (reine) would appear, all of this just before going at treetop level over the Gulf of Tonkin. If all was undetected by this time, our 3 or 6 attacking UH-34 Deltas and our hovercrafts to pick up prisoners and the sick and wounded would all be at the same place at the same time. We would then be able to make out West Hanoi, the Alcatraz work area and the Citadel area. There was also a railway that ran south to north up to Rue de Le Nom Day, Rue meaning street in French. The railway was on the west side of Hao Lo prison, and the commandant's living quarters, a large chateau (French mansion), shared the east area with the Ho Chi Min tomb. Inside the Hilton, we only had vague reports of what was really inside. So after all this the undisclosed area, it had not been revealed to us where we would depart from.

Meanwhile, back at Onslow Beach, security was tighter than ever. After jumping out of the copters, we would have Huey gunships and F104-5s, plus other components to aid us. This was drilled into us every day. I was really getting some jumping time logged in, as was everyone else. Once we hit in the semi-darkness in and around the whole prison area, we were to have a detail kill the commandant, the whole family and anyone else around. This was to show the North Vietnamese how easy it was to kick their asses any time we wanted to.

Well, if we failed this mission, it wouldn't be from lack of training. Once we, the attacking group, stormed the large door in front of the prison's main gate by blowing it out with a 3.5 rocket launcher, we would be in. We figured with our superior air cover and attack choppers that once we fought our way in, we would get every living prisoner (POW) out of there and onto hovercraft to safety. So after going through this by rehearsal, we had every damned thing down pat, except what we would really find inside the joint. When we got there, we figured on some very weak, dying, or near dead people in chains and dungeons. Only my imagination could tell me more. We were getting apprehensive about this mission. Every Marine knew once inside, they, the Vietcommies, would have the prison guarded to the teeth. There were also guard towers with tremendous fire power. Once we hit the ground, we had to knock them out or we would get mowed down like fish in a barrel because we would be right in front of them. They were bound to hear us coming and prepare with everything they could throw at us, including the kitchen sink.

We rehearsed our escape out of there with as many POWs that could walk, crawl, run or be stretchered out. These were the big questions: How many inside? How many could the large choppers that came with us accommodate? How many might be shot down waiting during the rescue? Mind-boggling and nightmarish thoughts ran through our minds. Could we really pull this off? Also, our maps told us there was a large garrison of NVA stationed within a mile of there. They no doubt had everything at their disposal because we would be fighting and killing them in their own backyard. Also, supposing everything went like clockwork, we had every POW loaded up and we were on our way down south, we

66.

knew they had air batteries nearby that could shoot us down in short order, even with our air cover bombing and strafing them. Well, on paper it looked great, a piece of cake, no sweat, you are some of the nation's finest, you cannot fail, you will not fail, you are too invincible to fail. These men have to be released—it's your sworn duty to get them out.

Some peace of mind: 1st Force, 2nd Force, 3rd Force, and 5th Force Recons overseas bound personnel were designated. The other Force Recons returning Stateside would make up 2nd and 1st Force: 2nd Force at Camp Geiger, North Carolina, 1st Force at Del Mar, California and 5th Force would be at Las Pulgas Camp Pendleton, California. So we, the 3rd Force Recon, were the outfit picked to do the job. We were elated, or shocked. Well, for damned sure we were trained for the mission. It was to be called SNAFU, which means all screwed up. This was to throw off any suspicion from us as far as VC or NVA radio reports were concerned—after all who would ever pick a name like SNAFU—that would be stupid. We got all our gear and available manpower together, and we said our good-byes, but not where we were going.

We C-130 aircrated our way to El Toro, California, MAW (Marine Air Wing), then we were trucked to Las Pulgas for billeting. Under strict secrecy, we worked in an identical facility at Del Mar, California. The Del Mar Hanoi Hilton area was identical to the one at Onslow Beach, North Carolina. We did the same parachuting, storming the gate, and routine. Everything from forcing guards to open cell doors, to releasing POWs out of the prison, and shooting our way out to safety—if this is what we'll find when we get there. The brass thought we were ready. We had covered every possible trouble spot that the experts planning this could imagine. The casualty loss was set low—we expected to hit them before they could react. This is what the planners counted on. If we pulled this off, we could all write our own tickets— the sky would be the limit. The Hanoi Hilton would be no longer holding POWs but would have a lot of dead, shot-up guards.

We went into more practice of piano wire killing, garroting, etc.—ways to take out sentries quietly using the silencer when and where needed. I thought of us jumping in and a song went through my mind that we had learned at special forces warfare school, "All I want to be is an airborne ranger, stand in the door, and jump into danger." We got our orders to head for Okinawa, so the whole 5th Force and men from 2nd Force and 1st Force joined us in our flight. As soon as we hit Guam, we fueled up. We stopped once also in Hawaii on the way to Okinawa. It seemed like a long flight. We had five C-130 aircraft flying in our formation. After hours and hours in the air, we landed at Cadena Air Force Okinawa Base. We then formed the famous 3rd Force Recon.

About two months before we got to the Rock, I got married to a lady who was working in a bar at the enlisted club at main side Camp Pendleton. She had one boy and one girl by another Marine who had been KIA (killed in action) in Vietnam. We were married at Carlsbad, California. Her kids were only a year or two old. I figured if I bought the farm, she would be the one to receive the money from the government. I seemed to have forgotten one thing, my father was still my original beneficiary and I hadn't changed the old will. Well, so much for wills. I wrote Joan, my wife, and told her we had landed in Okinawa, and we were forming a unit. I could not say any more than that. We trained up in the NTA in a mock build-up special area, again, very similar to what the other two were like at Onslow Beach, North Carolina, and Del Mar, California. This was high priority stuff. We were visited by the colonel in charge, and he told us what we were up against. It did not sound good at all.

At that time, all they had were air recon photos of some of the layout. We all looked these photos over close. We were also set up with cameras on our attack choppers to take pictures of our mission. The air cover would have cameras also. When I look back now, things were pretty primitive then.

Liberty call Four Corners, Kosa Sukiran, Okinawa: fight, make love, drink and be merry. Our outfit numbered about 100 men that were hand picked for SNAFU. Our liberty lasted the weekend in Okinawa. It never changes, it just gets better. It was too cold for the snakes to be a problem. After a week, the colonel thought we had it all honed down to perfection. After all, the more time taken up, the better chance this would leak out. So we said sayonara to the bar girls. We packed all our gear and trucked to Cadena AFB, Okinawa. Our five C-130s first landed in Tan Son Nhut where we fueled up, took on other personnel, and hauled north for Da Nang. Upon reaching Da Nang, we fell out in ranks and were assigned hooches. Seven of the eight people I was with originally were no longer with me. They were somewhere in the same area, because I saw them on occasion.

We heard that a group of our special trained people had been ambushed on a patrol somewhere around Dong Ha. I heard they had really taken some losses. Well, we were here on a special mission, let's get this over with and do it. There had been originally 6 to 8 UH-34 Deltas planned to take part in the raid. Now, with some of our highly trained people killed in action, we were down to 3 UH-34 Deltas with 12 men each: 36 people, not counting supporting elements. One of our other planes had stopped at PI at Clark AFB to refuel. We were overjoyed to see them when they joined us at Da Nang. They were saddened to hear of our losses through the critical ambush.

Chapter 7

That night early, down comes the word. We were informed again of the objective of the operation. We were divided into 3 13-man SRD (search, rescue and destroy) teams to attempt to rescue the downed flyers. Just outside Hanoi, North Vietnam, our teams were quickly loaded on to UH-34 Delta helicopters. The pilots were flying low to avoid constant gun batteries and radar. Approximately 0430 the 24th of December 1966, we were almost there. The pilots noted the terrain features and landmarks, all of a sudden it shot into view. The pilots gave us the green light, we jumped as soon as we hit the targets.

We encountered intense, hostile fire. We fought our way into the compound; about half of our force was machine gunned down outside the prison. I heard later on that the commandant and his family had been killed by our boys. Apparently, our intelligence had been inadequate. We met with extensive, heavy resistance from an enemy that outnumbered us at least 40 to 1. They had heavy, 51-caliber machine guns just raking us to pieces. Everyone except myself in my team was killed. When I hit the ground, I had first hit a wall. As I lay with the breath knocked out of me, a Vietcommie tried to bayonet me on the ground but another Marine shot him down before he could kill me.

Once inside the prison, we fought from floor to floor (3 floors) looking in the cells. I was aware of many freshly killed bodies. Blood pools on the floor, many bodies hung by their ankles, tortured and butchered. We observed approximately 250 individuals in one area and as we broke into a large compound, we saw another group of American airmen who had been systematically tortured, mutilated, and killed. In still another room, we found 100 men up on meat hooks, like butchered meat, and a large pit with dogs, where dead bodies and dismembered parts had been thrown to be eaten by the savage dogs. To gain entry to the main gate, we used a 3.5

rocket launcher to demolish the front door to the prison, killing about 20 guards, splattering them all over.

Additional guards came down the stairs shooting at us. We threw fragmentation grenades, blowing them all over the place. We lost five people going through the gate. The men to both my right and left were covered with blood. The gun battle inside was very intense. After getting inside, we slipped on the blood and entrails of the freshly killed POWs. The enemy had heard us coming and just shot every man in his chains. We could tell that all the POWs had been shot the same time, within 10 minutes. We received at least five grenades from NVA guards, and we had to throw grenades back to eliminate them. It was a cat-and-mouse situation. Slugs and fragments coming from all directions at once, and you couldn't see for shit in the dimly lit hallways. On the first floor we caught a North Vietnamese colonel. One of our team members asked him in Vietnamese, "Where are all the other POWs? Where?" The colonel said, "Screw you, GI," and we shot him when he tried to escape. We received a shower of grenades and lost four more men. One of our men finished them off with a grenade, blowing himself up while stopping the attackers. I stepped around a corner and was blown back by grenade concussions. We fought down the stairs fighting hand to hand. I was fighting a Vietcommie who had an unloaded rifle. He was trying to beat me with it. When I threw him over the stairwell, he fell maybe 60 feet. There were dead prisoners' bodies all around hanging from meat hooks like animals in a slaughter house. An NVA soldier grabbed me around the legs and tripped me. I was stabbed in the right side by another NVA with a trench knife. I had to kill him by putting my fingers in his eyes, and pushing my fingers into his skull. The team proceeded up the stairs, where we discovered yet another dog pit. The dogs could nearly jump out of it, there were so many bones in it.

We continued fighting by fire and maneuver, backed by our M-60 machine gun fire, during which time we saw more dead American bodies freshly killed—shot while chained to the walls. Some had entire magazines of AK47 (20) rounds unloaded in them. All the time I could hear throughout the prison mini-fire arms going on, it seemed like fireworks all exploding at once. Meanwhile, we, what was left of us, advanced.

On the second floor, we encountered four Russian advisors (torture technicians). They had rifles, knives, razors, and axes. One threw a hand axe at me, and it stuck in the stock of my M-14. I shot him down. They also had other implements of torture on them. We found an American colonel. They had the poor bastard stretched over hot coals. He had literally been melted to death. Needless to say, we shot the rest of the Russians. It was great pleasure.

On the third floor, we came under intense, small arms through cracks. We blew them up with our 3.5 rocket launchers using high explosives. I received wounds in the buttocks, scrotum, left thigh, and femur. We lost two additional people going down the stairs.

On the ground, we encountered withering fire, incoming mortar fire. We called F-105 air, my radio operator was killed, air strikes were almost right on our position. I could see helicopters being shot down in the distance at this time. I was hit by a grenade fragment in the neck which penetrated my left cheek, knocked out 12 teeth, and came out of my forehead. I was carrying an injured airman over my shoulder at the time of my injury. AK-47 rounds passed through his body killing him and hitting me. I was running towards the copter—the only survivor.

While the copter waited to take off, the pilot said, "Get some 105 air on those trucks coming." I looked and could see about 60 trucks loaded with troops. I also saw some of our own guys being chased in front of the trucks. The jet dove before we could call on the radio to the pilot. Automatically, like he had read our minds, he dropped napalm all over them, but also hitting the people who were running ahead of the trucks.

Meanwhile, the co-pilot was dying, and the pilot was

wounded. The people running ahead of those trucks could have been POWs or some of our guys, perhaps prison details. I will never know now. As far as using the radio to call in air on those trucks, it was almost impossible for me to even whisper with the loss of my teeth.

As we were lifting off, a Marine came running as hard as he could, but he was shot down in the middle of the field about 50 yards from us. The pilot was airborne and we were taking 51-caliber machine gun fire like we were a sieve. We kept getting hit through the floor. I got hit in both ankles. The co-pilot was now dead, and the other pilot was dying. They had caught some rounds through the doors and sides of the bird till the copter looked like a shotgun blast had penetrated every inch of the copter. As we got airborne, we shot up and away. My M-14 rifle that was slung over my back slipped down my waist, hit the floor of the chopper, and went out the door. Two or three of the support helicopters were shot down by coastal batteries, and two F-105 aircraft were shot down. The flack was so heavy you could get out and walk on it. We were vibrating and shaking to pieces. We were losing altitude while on automatic pilot and we were on fire.

Miraculously, the pilot, before he died, had set us on a viable course and we flew for hours it seemed. Gradually gliding downward. The shrapnel in my buttocks, legs, and ankles was hurting me bad. And my mouth was driving me crazy. By this time, I realized our supporting elements, such as the hovercraft and gun ships, were either shot down or had escaped. I now knew both these pilots were dead, and I was heading for some jungle. We crashed into triple canopy jungle treetops, upside down. I was thrown out the door roughly 75 to 100 feet. One of the dead pilots came down with me, I broke both ankles in the fall.

An enemy patrol came double-timing my way looking for the downed helicopter. There were several Russian Spetznatz and Russian Commandos with them. They began shooting about 150 yards away; they were firing RPG (Russian propelled grenades) at the copter still burning in the tree top. I crawled into a ditch full of water. I could hear the enemy looking for the helicopter crew. I saw Russians and North Vietnamese regulars, chopping the one dead pilot into pieces with their machetes. The other pilot burned in the wreckage. The enemy patrol used white phosphorus grenades to find me. A small piece of shrapnel bounced off a tree, landing in the middle of my back. I still have a large scar there today.

Meanwhile, the leeches were feeding on me, and I was in a state of shock. I kept hearing a tune we had learned during training. It went like this, "If I die on the Russian front, bury me on top of a Russian cunt." I was thinking what a great job of storming the Hanoi Hilton we did! Well, I said to myself, "What a hell of a mess I'm in now." I kept thinking maybe someone besides me escaped. It was getting dark, and I made a hobble stick to lean on. I crossed a road. There was a lot of traffic on it and they had been filling in bomb craters. All kinds of new construction work was being done. I managed to crawl past a patrol that was just going out. They were all real gung ho and double-timed themselves into formation.

They were no doubt alerted to try and find whoever escaped from that shot-down copter. I ran into a stream and found a small boat. I started floating south when I ran into heavy reeds. I would stop during the early morning, and lay up all day hiding. The Commie Viets were everywhere. They didn't miss a trick. They almost caught me on two other occasions. I was midstream and they shot my boat up. It practically sunk right from beneath me. I had to swim under water to a dock area to get away. Luckily, it was at night. I didn't have a clue where I was.

On top of the dock was a parked car, a 1940 Packard, I think. Inside this car there were two people making out. It was an NVA captain and his girlfriend. I had my 45 pistol trained on them. The woman was exhorting the man to kill me if they had the chance. They could see I was really hurt. I forced him to give me some first aid, and he put a splint on my left leg. All the while, the bitch is saying in Vietnamese, "Kill him! jump him!" but the Dia Uy (captain) stayed cool. He knew I would shoot him and his girlfriend ASAP if he messed up. Meanwhile, I almost passed out from the pain.

I then had the woman tie up the captain and gag him. I didn't know what to do with her. I had her cover the captain over with brush. The car's gas tank was on empty, so that was out. So at gun point, I had her drag out a row boat and she rowed me out into the current. It was getting pitch black, the darker the better. I traveled at night and would hide during the day. Well, around 0400 hours, I started to black out with pain. I kept hearing that training song again, "All I want to be is an airborne recon ranger, stand in the door and jump into danger." All of a sudden, a big liner almost ran us over. I kept asking her, "Where the hell are we? What port are we near?" She didn't understand a word I was saying, and she kept pointing back towards shore. So I motioned to her to go back towards land, we must have covered a lot of water because I could hear aircraft and explosions somewhere south. I was using the stars, the big dipper, as my reference point.

Then here comes this NVA gun boat. They went right by us without seeing us. The woman started to scream her head off. She dove over the side and I saw her go under. It was still pre-dawn and really dark. I don't think the woman could swim a stroke. She probably thought the gun boat would see her, pick her up, and capture me. They say the good Lord protects those in dire peril. Well, he was really looking out for this poor old soul. It was almost light. I floated into shore and more reed cover. I didn't know then that I was only a short distance from the DMZ shoreline. I came across friendly forces—ARVN advisors, and some Marines from the 7th Regiment. At first, I had a hell of a time convincing them that I wasn't a Soviet bloc agent.

Finally, I was medivaced to Da Nang at Da Nang hospital. Hospital personnel discovered that I was wounded many times. Due to the lack of publicity concerning this operation, I believe the entire operation, the death, the torture of many Americans was covered up and never reported or accounted for. I was given an account of my many wounds as follows. This is a full record of wounds I received during my week in enemy country.

Sergeant Koski was brought into this field hospital in Da Nang SV Nam into surgical with extensive wounds to his left jaw, loss of teeth, wounds in face and head, bayonet wounds to right side of body, shrapnel/frags in both ankles, left ankle appears fractured, multiple fragment wounds, left ankle and right ankle stab wound, right leg and left femur broken, extensive shrapnel wounds in left chest, left neck. 14 teeth missing or broken off, tongue partially severed, fragments exiting from left cheek, left forehead, right ankle appears fractured also, shrapnel left thigh, left knee, shrapnel both hands, right and left buttocks, foreskin ripped, explosion flash in both eyes, temporary medical treatment applied, patient is conscious with considerable loss of blood. Treatment X-ray probe Sergeant Koski, being treated for severe broken right ankle, recommend pins, temp 100 degrees, pulse—rapid, substantial work up for gun shot wound coming out of forehead.

A doctor there said, "Hey, Marine! your right leg has to be removed at the thigh." In the corner of the ward, I noticed a pile of arms, hands, and legs six feet high, piled up next to a wall. I had a 45-caliber pistol in my shoulder holster. I drew it out and told him if he came near me, I would blow his head off and anyone else with the same idea in mind. He said "You are crazy! Let us take it off and we'll send you home. No more war for you, and also you have a gangrene infection in it. You will die if it is not removed." I said, "No! Get away from me." Six hours later I was on my way to Camp Kuhe U.S. Army Hospital in Okinawa. There they saved my leg.

One day in 1985, I was at the San Francisco VA Hospital, at Fort Miley, and I ran into this same doctor. He said, "You still have your right leg?"

I said, "Yes." He seemed very nervous and surprised. I said, "I am damn glad you never took it off." The question is, how many legs and arms were amputated needlessly?

From Okinawa, I ended up at Balboa Naval Hospital, San Diego, California. While at Camp Kuhe, I was debriefed by a Major USMC type and several senior NCOs from Naval intelligence. Their remarks were, "Don't worry, Sergeant Koski, this episode will be taken care of." I found out later that I was recommended for the Medal of Honor. This mission was classified and kept secret all these years, even to the point where this mission was never disclosed, and finally the documents were shredded. I didn't know this until 1994 when I found out about all the shredding of secret POW documents. In 1994, we had evidence to back up all these statements.

Well, getting back to Balboa U.S. Naval Hospital. They soon got me back on my feet again. After Okinawa and San Diego Hospitals, I was sent home to convalesce in another atmosphere. My wife, Joan, was delighted to see my progress in healing up. It was a pleasure to be in our house on Alturas Street in Fallbrook, California. This was just back of the main side Camp Pendleton gate. I was up for Staff Sergeant/E-6 and I was a combat veteran of two tours in Vietnam. I had the world in my hands, and a downhill pull. Well, Joan was pretty sick all the time with asthma, and the boy, Bobbie, was 3 1/2, ad the girl, Crystal, was 2 1/2. We had to make a decision to stay in the Corps or get out. My 6-year enlistment was over in May 1967, so instead of shipping over and making Staff Sergeant, I took an Honorable Discharge and left for Washington D.C.

We worked for my sister Ria who owned a grocery store. We lived upstairs from her for three years. She was living in Maryland with her husband and their four kids. In 1968 during the Tet Offensive, my brother Duane and my cousin Ted were both killed in action at Hue City, South Vietnam. They were both Marines, Hue was between Camp Evans in the North, and Phu Bai in the South. I heard they were both being dusted off when the evacuation copter was destroyed in the air. Oh well, dear brother and cousin, I got a few for you to make up for it all. Rest well until we meet another day.

Meanwhile, while Joan was in Indiana visiting her mother, she died. Her mother and sister took the kids and moved to Florida. After that I lived at my sister Ria's place. The grocery store was burned to a certain extent during the 1968 Washington, D.C., riots. Ria sold the store and she and her husband got jobs as high school teachers. I took a job selling home products door to door. I was working in Falls Church, Virginia, and living in Oxon Hill, Maryland. I met a lady named Carla, and we got married in 1971. At this time I was thinking to myself, why not go back into the Corps? The war was still raging and the Corps needed guys like me with past experience. So I went up to Baltimore, Maryland, and ran into an old friend of mine, a Master Sergeant Tuson, USMC. He said, "What the hell are you doing alive? I read your death certificate, and your old man collected 10 grand only to have to pay it back when they found out you were still alive. Why did you ever get out? You should have shipped over and you would be at least my rank now."

Well, I told him that Joan was scared that I might be

sent over a third time, and that she thought it was too risky to stay in the Corps. So we got out, and I had hated myself every day since. "Well," he said, "what can I do for you?" As he was a Marine Corps recruiter with a lot of pull, I said, "Send me back to the monsoons again." He said, "Can you pass these mental and physical tests? If you can, I'll get you orders for 'Nam." Well, I passed all the tests and finished the exams in one day. I got a 95 on the mental tests, and they let me through on the physical. So I got orders for good ole Camp LeJeune. We called it "Swamp Lagoon". It was like old times back to Onslow Beach, and this time it was BN, Recon.

Chapter 8

I met all kinds of my old friends there. They had all been promoted to gunnery sergeants and above. I now had many friends in high places. I met Master Gunnery Sergeant Charlie Campbell. He said "Live at my place at Topsail Beach, North Carolina, and drive back and forth to work," so I moved in with him. I discovered that he and his wife were divorced. In four months' time I was really getting in shape running and swimming. Captain Gangle and I were good friends, and I made some fast promotions from PFC to Lance Corporal. After all, Recon was my trade.

Well, the day I was waiting for arrived. We were told to fall into a company formation. The 1st sergeant said, "All Vietnam Vets one step backward," which we did. He said, "All Vets have orders for a NATO (Norway, Germany, Sweden, Finland, and Denmark) cruise with the 6th U.S. Naval Fleet. Well, blow me down, it's Vietnam for the new guys, and a NATO cruise for us. We trained day and night, swimming missions, scouting, and patrolling. One night while we were inserting swimmers into a rough ocean, the signals somehow got mixed up in the roar of the choppers. Five men jumped about 100 feet above water because of accidentally misunderstood orders from the Dive Master. Instead of "go", the order was "no".

Part of every swimmer's standard gear was coral shoes, flippers, and a mask with snorkel attached over his arm. When you made chopper inserts, you also had the gray trunks and knife with flares on a belt. As soon as you hit the water you put on your flippers and snort mask, and got ready to swim to shore. When that accident happened, we only found one body, a Corporal Black, USMC. The rest of them we never found. The usual height for an insert into the water from a moving copter is about 25 feet in the air, not 100 feet. The CO really raised hell about people being killed in training missions. We looked for them all that night, and for the next three days. No bodies were found; the tide, currents and undertow had gotten them. The Atlantic Ocean and all the swamp inlets were treacherous because of quicksand, cottonmouths, and rattlesnakes.

There were four lucky other guys who had not jumped in with them. They had been in front of the door, and had heard the word "no" instead of the word "go", and as a result had not made the mistake of jumping. This had saved the four men's lives. Water inserts are bad enough at 25 feet in daylight, let alone at 100 feet in the dark. I used to hate fast moving choppers because when you jumped, your belly really flopped hard. The water was like cement. It was tough to regain your senses and put on your flippers and snorkel mask and then to get organized with your swim team. After all of this, you had to swim against a terrific current.

We lost another man a week later. The radio man who had a radio strapped to his back was knocked out of the boat, a light rubber craft, and was drowned. He could not get his quick release to work, and the heaviness of the radio weighted him down. the other three men dove after him, but the waterway inlet had been dredged for big boats. It was too dark, deep, and murky to see him. They found him a week later washed out of the mouth of the waterway. In spite of our training, and our real good physical condition, sometimes everything went horseshit wrong. When they found his body, the quick releases were still stuck—something quick releases are never supposed to do.

Well, they passed the word to pack our gear. We were going on a NATO cruise. We loaded up on a big carrier, the Oriskany, a helo hauler. There were choppers on the top deck of every size and description. We were 2nd Recon BN, attached to the 6th Marines. We would be used if there was any swimming or jumping to do. After being out to sea a few days, we encountered Russian subs behind us and saw their listening trawlers within our range of eyesight. We were a big convoy, so we refueled at sea. We stopped at the Azores to pick up more ships, and finally the fiords of Norway began to meet us. We had been at sea now for weeks, and land was in our sight. We finally arrived at Bergen, Norway, where we pulled a hammer anvil. We were only a few miles from the Russian border, and we could see the Reds across the border.

During the operation, one of our birds (choppers) carrying our BN, Chaplain and the Regiment XO and other observers was spotlighting its way down a mountainside, when it hit the mountain with a prop and blew up. They brought the wreck aboard ship, and there were 12 killed on it. After a while, the wreck reeked of death from the body parts smashed on the metal.

Bergen, Norway, was a fiord port fishing city. After we pulled liberty there for two or three nights, they started putting up signs in English saying "No Americans Allowed," referring to Marines and sailors. There were a lot of fights going on, so the ships CO (commanding officer) said to secure all liberty because of the complaints they had been receiving about fighting Norwegians. We were there about two more days, said goodbye to the liberty boats, and left for Oslo, Norway.

I met a girl named Gerd while I was there. We wrote a few letters, but I was married so it ended. The next fiord we saw was the one leading into Oslo. This was a liberty cruise, so we put on our uniforms, loaded into liberty boats and discovered Oslo. We had a week of port and starboard liberty. Americans were getting mighty unpopular in Oslo. There were a lot of fights, and the Russians seemed to influence these people to no end. Norway was a North Atlantic Treaty Organization (NATO), but their men resented us around their women, and our cultures refused to blend. Some of them spoke fair English, but it was just enough for us to have a misunderstanding. They kept bringing up the World War II occupation with Germany.

We saw a village square in Bergen that had been the scene of a firing squad massacre. Many Norwegians had been stood up against the wall and shot there. This was around 1942-1943. We were wearing our green winter uniforms, and some guys had had sharpshooter badges on, which are almost identical to the German iron cross. They were up in arms and at odds with us as soon as they saw this sharpshooter badge being worn by some of our people. Sharpshooter is one level below expert rifle. Well, we partied and had a great time there. After all, we were representing the USA as ambassadors of good will.

We got back aboard ship and hauled ass for Helsinki, Finland. Once we arrived we were greeted like kings. We spent a night in Sweden, and three days in Copenhagen, Denmark. This cruise was real fun. We got along well with these people. The men didn't give a rats ass who you went out with. Now I call that friendly. We left a good impression there. One Saturday morning the ship EXO said, "Stand by to leave, we are going to Germany." So off we sailed again, saying goodbye to all. Just as our fleet got into the North Sea we hit a terrible storm. The big carrier we were on was almost capsized in the gigantic waves and troughs. About 12 ships in our fleet sank that night. It was the Navy's birthday, October 1972.

The storm got so bad that we were walking on the bulkheads of the ship instead of the decks. Water was running ankle deep from the heads. Everyone was seasick. We couldn't walk without having to hold onto a hammock or some other object. When we were in the galley, our trays would slide away from us. We had to hold onto our own trays and cups. The captain of the ship came over the ship's intercom and said, "I advise you all to pray to God, as we are on the verge of losing the ship. Only the gods will save us now." By some miracle, God saved us. About a third of the copters and around 40 of the ship's crew were washed overboard. The next day it cleared up. As we pulled into Wilhelmshaven, Germany, we found that there were 12 ships lost at sea, and numerous lives lost. They never told us exactly how many. We pulled a parachute jump on our next mission in Oldenburg, Germany. We had four days of liberty, so

83.

we made the most of it, although our German wasn't all that great.

Some of us knew quite a bit of German, so we made out ok. One night on our way to the Autobahn, we had a talk with the cab driver. He was a veteran of the battle of Britain and had been a pilot on several missions as a Heinkle bomber pilot, I met a lot of interesting people while there. The Germans drink their beer warm, and we got loaded fast on warm beer, especially on an *Oktoberfest.* One night we didn't have liberty and we were dry for a drink, so after diving off the back of the ship, I swam about one mile and mistakenly bought twelve quarts of cooking wine in a Chinese food store. I put the wine in my swim tow bag and returned to the ship. We hardly noticed the difference, it was still alcohol. The weather was still warm there, so on our next liberty, we really got drunk. We got a cab driver all pissed off. He hauled us all over the place and we couldn't pay him any marks because we were shit-faced and broke. He finally accepted two of our government swim watches as payment and drove away happy, so we didn't have any MP trouble.

Once again it was time to bid fond farewells, and in the meantime we started our long cruise back to the USA. Every time we left a country, we exchanged their currency for ours. Well, here I am back in the Corps working my way up through the ranks again. It's hard to have been a sergeant once and then five years later start all over from scratch. It took us weeks to get back to Stateside, when we arrived it was cold weather, we had just returned to Onslow beach. When the 1st sergeant said, "I need a person over 76 inches tall, with a combat action ribbon for starters. This person will have to pass the security clearance and report within five working days to guess where. U.S. Marine barracks Washington D.C.." This is the showcase of the U.S. Marine Corps, only the elite are selected. I was delighted, but at the same time, I felt sorry for leaving the FMF.

I had been staying at Charlie Campbell's house at

Topsail Beach, North Carolina. He and I had been sergeants (E-5) together back in 1966, now he was a master gunnery sergeant (E-9), and I was an E-3. Well, we were great friends, and Charlie had heard I'd rejoined the corps to return back to Vietnam. Charlie is also an airborne, scuba, recon, ranger etc.. I had told him I was trying for an overseas bound rifle company, and he said, "Look, you have done your bit, now enjoy Washington D.C." Meanwhile Carla, my wife, was down at Charlie's place too. She had brought a girlfriend down for him and they really hit it off. The next day was a very emotional day. Charlie had the Navy Cross from Vietnam for heroics and courage. That was the last day I ever saw him. Well, Carla and I headed back for Alexandria, Virginia, where we had an apartment. So here I was, already living in Virginia and stationed at the Marine barracks. Talk about having it made.

Or I thought I had it made. I had orders for MCI Co. (Marine Corps Institute Company). I knew this was good duty. Don't get shit canned from here. The first thing was get measured for three suits of dress blues, getting issued your ribbons and metals Anodized all the medals and brass belt tips, scuba head, jump wings, and silver plate buckles. So no matter how much you sweat on your brass or how bad the humidity, your brass always looked sharp. We had a press shop at our disposal, so we had our uniforms with sharp creases looking top drawer, and our barracks covered the bills. Our shoes were coraform or a built-in shine to the leather material. Our trousers and gloves were white. All utility uniforms were winter green, summer short-sleeved tropical shirts, and piss cutters, undressed blues, every piece of uniform was cut down to size; nothing baggy was ever worn aboard the barracks. When you reported for duty you were squared away. It took about two months for the sew shop to taper your uniforms. Just so, once this was completed, you were expected to stay squared away to the max, not a thread out of place or a wrinkle anywhere.

One month after I reported in to MCI Co., 1st

Sergeant Bradley called me in. He said, "You are not an office worker, you are an ex-Force Recon man, and you are also Marine Corps physical fitness trained and graduated from the Henderson Hall School." I said, "Aye, Sir." He said, "We are sending you over to H and S (Headquarters and Service Co.). You will be their fitness instructor." I was promoted to Corporal E-4 about two months later. Well, my main duty was PTing the poor souls who happened to be in my charge. We would run around the city, stopping and doing push-ups, and then head for Bolling AFB Washington, D.C., for pull-ups and sit-ups.

I was considered part of the special services detail. Our duties were to also show movies to the troops once a week. Corporal Jim O'Malley and I also issued out all sorts of athletic equipment. We were in the old barracks built in 1801. Our area was up in a screened-in loft, where we kept all our athletic gear. Every 4 months the Corps runs the PFT (Physical Fitness Test), consisting of 20 underhand pull-ups, eighty sit-ups, done under 3 minutes, and numerous other exercises including a 3-mile run with a time limit.

Every Marine in every outfit throughout the whole Marine Corps does this every four months, rain, snow, sleet, wind, or shine. No one is ever overlooked unless he is on light duty or no duty and as soon as that person is able and back on full duty, he runs the PFT. Well, we oversaw this, as well as athletic events. And we prepared athletic fields for games, like chalk marking the field lines, etc.. Anything to do with athletics and we were involved. Sometimes we were really busy, other times not. Meanwhile I'd drive home every night and report back into the barracks at 0700 hours. I would eat breakfast there, and the seven of us in Special Services would prepare for the day's events. Every company had a duty NCO roster so at least once a month, we would stand the "dirty duty", as it was named. This meant up all night and no sleep, and continue on the next day, with no sleep had the night before. in the uniform of the day, which was greens,

The U.S. Marine Corps Commandant's dog, Chesty, was mascot at all the Thursday and Friday night parades and all other celebrations that the U.S. Marine band and barracks had. The U.S. Marine Corps band was and is world renowned, so Chesty the purebred bulldog was a favorite at all attractions. Chesty was the name of every bulldog that had been mascot since the time of General Chesty Puller USMC. General Puller had won eight Navy Crosses and was an ex-U.S. Marine Corps Commandant. In fact, the current commandant has his quarters at the north end of the parade field, where commandants have resided since 1801. When I was there at special services, a Sergeant K. Gardner and Corporal James O'Malley were in charge of the dog walking during the parades. Chesty wore a World War I helmet with the U.S. Marine Corps insignia and a dog vest with USMC on it. And his rank sometimes changed. Chesty would relieve himself in public and he would be demoted a stripe. This would go into his official service record book.

The dog had a service record book, just as all Marines had. When I was there, from 1973-76, we kept the same dog. He was in good health, and when you would exercise him, he would tackle you and play very rough. He would try to jump on you and knock you down. What could you expect from a canine who was taught from a pup to develop military bearing? As the dog was trained, sometimes it developed a temper, but all in all this Chesty was a good mannered dog. Some of the parades we had would require the dog to stand at attention for up to five minutes at a time. A parade is a real spectacle to behold with silent drill teams and fixed bayonets doing the marching manual.

Whenever a dignitary died, the body bearers escorted the person to his or her final resting place at Arlington National Cemetery. I was there during the Nixon years and the Ford years. When Nixon was having his Watergate problems, we had to fall out with full combat gear to train for riot control. They thought he might be impeached and our job was to keep people away from the

White House who were hostile. Well, I picked up sergeant again, and my job was to escort couples to various seats during parades on Thursday and Friday nights. This was a "made in the shade" job. I was walking around escorting high ranking officers and their wives or girlfriends. When I pulled this duty I wore dress blues with medals, jump wings, and scuba head, along with all my campaign ribbons on the right side of my uniform and medals on the left, with the gold jump wings being the most senior on top of all else. After parades, everyone would go to their respective clubs at the south end of the barracks. Sometimes we were invited to the officers clubs, and took our wives or girlfriends along with us. Everybody just got smashed. Most of the officers knew us, and each other well, but there was still that old military restriction where you didn't speak until spoken to. There was no chance for familiarity to breed contempt back in '73, you had to be a Vietnam veteran to be stationed there. However there were some exceptions that had never been overseas, just stationed there because they had to fill the roster quotas.

One night I was duty NCO and I was informed I would be relieved because my wife was having a baby at Walter Reed Hospital. This was January '73. When I got there, I was informed that the baby was stillborn. My wife, Carla, was supposed to have a C-section but the doctors who had followed her pregnancy had been sent elsewhere, and the new doctor did not have the charts; so the baby was delivered dead. It was an 11-pound girl.

Back at the barracks, I was informed that no one had been ordered to relieve me: like I had committed some kind of crime. This was cleared up later, as the officer of the day had made a mistake and not appointed another A-duty. So it wasn't my mistake or my fault. We tried to sue Walter Reed Hospital, but to no avail. This incompetency on a doctor's part later caused our divorce.

I started catching White House duty, and all I did was salute and open doors. This went on for about a year. I was working and rubbing elbows with the President and his whole staff. This was about as distinguished as you could get, and I met a lot of interesting people.

I was living at my Uncle Mike's house at 3320 South 6th St., Arlington, Virginia. Mike was a great old gentleman. He had served with the old Marine Corps back during the worst fighting in France. He had been wounded twice, decorated with the Silver Star, and still limped a good deal. Uncle Mike had been married five times, and all his wives had passed away. He had 20 grown kids and I don't know how many grand- and great-grandchildren. Mike was my mom's oldest brother.

One day the flag detail, in their hurry, put the storm rain flag on upside down. It wasn't noticed until later and everyone was busted. As punishment, they lost one stripe and were transferred elsewhere; probably to the FMF. Well then, I went down to the Quantico, Virginia, rifle range, and qualified as expert in rifle and 45 pistol. After I returned from the range, I was somewhat of a celebrity. Double expert. Everyone wanted that.

Another time, the civilian workers were tearing down an old section of wall that was built in 1801 and they found a skeleton. Somewhere in the dim past, a man had been murdered by being stabbed in the back. The knife was still in between the back and spine. He had the Marine greens on and a Sam Brown belt. After he was killed, persons unknown cemented his body into a walled-up closet. After all these years only a skeleton in tattered rags, and dust covered. Near as I know, even through his dental work, no one ever found his identity.

One day the grounds keepers waved me over to help them with a heavy pipe used to irrigate the grass. I was in civilian clothes, so I said to myself, "No problem." As we all lifted together they lost their footing and fell, I had all the weight then, and I fell backwards. I had to go to the hospital and they said I had an inguinal hernia. So I went from Walter Reed to Bethesda Naval Hospital to see a specialist. He said, "We can cut it in two, but you might have trouble later." So I still have it, and it bothers me at times.

About two years before I was stationed at the barracks, there was a murder down in the navy yard where the body bearers are billeted. A duty NCO was stabbed to death, and I think to this day it remains unsolved.

At the good old Navy yard in Washington, D.C., I had a dentist named Lt. Commander Gross USNR restore practically all my teeth over a three-year period. This restoration was from that Vietnam wound in the mouth from 1966. I still saw him until I moved.

Well, about 1975, the new barracks directly across the street south was completed. They had been building it for ten years. Now we moved new gear into a new building. I was having a painful time with my right ankle. I had been wounded there in '66 with a RPG rocket propelled grenade. It was swelling up the whole side of my right inner ankle. There was a piece of shrapnel lodged in the tarsal tunnel area of my heel and lower ankle, this is called "tarsal tunnel syndrome" . Well, an operation was done by the same surgeon who operated on my chronic planter fasciitis in 1965, a Captain Slemmons USN. At Camp Pendleton Naval Hospital, this latest operation was performed. It was 1975, and I was laid up about six months. In the meanwhile, they were living in the new barracks and the old barracks at 8th and I was still used by the musicians who did all their work there. The barracks CO's office stayed at the old barracks. The old barracks had a long, distinguished history. During the battle of 1812, the British tried to storm and capture it.

The siege went on for days to no avail. And during the Civil War, it was a Northern fortress. At that time, Washington, D.C., was a city in turmoil, because in the 1861-65 period the Civil War could have gone either way.

I was discharged from Bethesda Naval Hospital and returned to duty at the barracks in August 1976.

Chapter 9

I took an honorable discharge from there and got out again. In the back of my mind was Special Forces. Well, I was out, but I kept thinking, "Why not go in the Army and try something different?"

In 1977, I moved from my uncle's house to Greenbelt, Maryland. I had met Ruth at a party and we started going together. Uncle Mike liked her, too. We lived together for a while before getting married, (my third time), in West Virginia. I got a job with NASA Greenbelt security police and received my gun permit and all my security police uniforms and went through my training period. Once this was done I became a fulltime police security officer. There were about 25 posts to guard on the whole reservation.

We were in Prince George County, so we worked with the Prince George County police direct. There never was a lot of trouble while I was there, but then the captain of the guard liked his people to work a lot of double shifts. So sometimes after pulling eight hours you would find yourself starting another eight hours with no break in between. This kind of got old after a while, and working tired can get you killed. I had roving patrol one night, and after eight hours and starting another eight, I went to sleep at the wheel. I flipped the car over on some ice and back on its wheels again. There was deep snow everywhere, so I made a soft landing. A few dents and some oil leaked out, but I wasn't hurt, so I was very lucky it did not burn up or worse. Those Ford patrol cars were built rugged, and I made my report that it was the ice's fault. Well, the job was good, but very routine; we made up daily work reports at the end of each shift. We were actually working for the NASA Goddard Space Program, and our job was tight security aboard the reservation, from guarding bank payrolls to apprehending people who had snuck onto the grounds. We also checked all pedestrians and traffic for their I.D. cards that showed they worked there.

Ruth was working as a maid for a family in Greenbelt, and after work we would go to the local VFW and get tanked up. That was from August 1976 to May 1978, when I decided to join up with the 11th Special Forces 5th Pathfinder PLT. The 11th Special Forces Green Beret is located at Fort Meade, Maryland. They do only special forces work, and are deployable at any time. I talked to the Army recruiter, and he said, "Welcome home." Force Recon are our best people here, and they are very gung ho. Well, he looked over my DD-214 and saw I had completed all the schools for Special Forces while a Marine. So I kept my sergeant rank, and signed on for two years with Special Forces. So I just traded uniforms, and kept the same rank.

The 1st sergeant's office had a sign above the door, "No non-hackers allowed, only the best tread these grounds." Here, again, everyone ran everywhere they went. It was a complete replay of 2nd Force Recon's area. It was home away from home. It took a while to get onto the Army slogans, but all this came back to me fast. Like when you were dropped for push-ups at Fort Benning you always replied, "Clear, Sergeant Airborne." If you did not understand it was, "Not clear, Sergeant." The words "Marine Corps" was a no-no there. When I first walked into my barracks, and all over the post, I met seven ex-Force Recon men. It was like old times; this company I was in resembled the French Foreign Legion. We had people from every walk of life and other militaries around the world. You name a commando unit from somewhere in the world, and it could be found there in those ranks. A motley crew, but all dedicated combat vet professionals.

The first thing we did was get a crash course in flying all the helicopters and UH-10 fixed wing, resembling Piper Cubs, so if the pilots were shot up, we could still navigate to some kind of a landing. The first week we were forming up MOS's into squads into platoons from team level. Every day around garrison, we would be training for another war. So one Monday when I was off,

I collected my last paycheck from Goddard Space Finance Office. I had gone from the U.S. Marine barracks in D.C. to being a cop at Goddard, to Army Special Forces. Well, I don't have much to say about physical condition, because I was never feeling better. We were spending two weeks at a crack in the bush, and that was my MOS 11 Bush. So back to the days of sleeping on the ground, moving fast only under the cover of noise; and living off animals, snakes, and birds. A C-ration was considered a feast although we never saw any. Our job was like Recon, "Swift, Silent, and Deadly." I had a sergeant who was a DSC winner while serving with 5th Special Forces in 'Nam, so we compared a lot of notes together. He had always admired the USMC, so we really hit it off.

Well, somebody put up something on the "hot scoop" board that said, "Special warfare school in Panama Canal Zone." No one explained how we would get there, but we packed all needed gear and some T-10 olive drab parachutes that had just come by air drop from Fort Lee, Virginia. They had also dropped some heavy stuff like trucks and tanks by air, so the parachute riggers were really busy untangling shroud lines and repacking chutes. This was to be a company size operation. So Saturday about noon we had everything we needed and went off the runway at Andrews AFB, Maryland. We were in some kind of terrible rain storm with high winds. And when the green light went on the jump master hollered out "Stand up, hook up, sound off for equipment check, and stand in the door!" Well, I was the first paratrooper in the stick nearest the door, so I led the way. We were all jumping long general purpose bags and believe me, baby, what I saw out that door looked like the worst electrical storm I had ever seen. The plane I had just jumped out of was doing a tail spin, and seemed out of control in the terrible wind, rain, and lightening. This jump should have been aborted, but you hired out to be tough in this outfit. I checked canopy, I was open and drifting I knew not where. When you are jumping GP bags, it is customary to pull the quick release and about 50 feet of nylon rope and the bag just swings like a pendulum below you. If you are in trees or built-up city areas, you always ride it in. Otherwise, it can catch in a tree or light post and cut your head off. Great thought: no head. Or at least break your neck. Well, our drop zone was miles away and when I landed, I hit into a bunch of jungle on a tiny island and it was so dark I couldn't see a thing. It was real hot and steamy and my rigger's taped-on watch said: "0 dark hours in the night." I figured most of the jumpers behind me must have blown to somewhere close around me. We used the bird whistle to find each other. After it became light, I saw quicksand all around me. It was like a floating raft among bottomless quicksand. Well, the main objective was to creep up on a bunch of legs (non-jumpers), surprise and capture them. According to our map and compass we were about 10 miles off, and on the Columbian side.

After gathering up our teams and finding everyone in one piece, we planned our attack strategy. This area is the most notorious area in the world for snakes, panthers, mosquitoes as big as wasps, crocodiles, and you name it. Special Forces warfare training was a good name for it. One corporal was caught high in a tree, so he let his reserve parachute drop and hit his quick release box on his main harness and went hand over hand downward. This is a surefire way to get out of a high tree or any high object you are hanging from. After all, an enemy patrol could see you there for miles. Escape and keep moving is the key to staying alive.

Well we finally reached Panama, we slid by the border sentries like snakes, they never even looked up. So from Columbia to Panama and so on with the training. They had choppers and patrols out looking for us, but they just walked or flew over us without even knowing they were close. We took an entire platoon and captured two choppers and crews, all our prisoners after the three-week stay in the swamps of Panama. Colón, the major city nearest by, became our liberty spot for two days. We had one man who was bit by a Bushmaster and died. The place was infested by crocodiles. It's a plain wonder we didn't have more people killed or mauled.

Colón was a real wild place and the cops didn't even show up. When there was a fight or trouble, we had some permanent personnel from nearby bases who thought they owned the broads and clubs, but we soon showed them the error in their ways. While we were in the Zone we met a lot of other Americans, some of them had lived there all their lives, because they had been stationed there a long time.

We flew back to Andrews AFB and unpacked and went back to Fort Meade, Maryland. It was good to get back. I went down to Greenbelt. I saw the wife and we went down to Oxon Hill, Maryland, to check out my sister and her husband Bob. By this time she had six kids—two by her first husband, and the rest by Bob. She also had Teddy Bear, a big German shepherd dog. He was a good watch dog, and during the riots of 1968 kept the rioters away from the store we operated, just by his presence. We got one fire bomb through the window, but, all in all, the store was saved. Stan, her first husband, had received the store from his father, so the store had been in the family for about 30 years. The old man still ran one in Alexandria, Virginia, then he retired.

Well, we settled down at Beret Headquarters, as we called it, and waited for the next operation to be planned. So they then planned another operation, this time it was up in Fort Francis Ontario, Canada. We were jumped into the wilds of the Canadian border by tailgate C-130. It was fall and mighty cold. We went in as 4 teams of 4; 16 all total. It was about 20 below zero and really cold. We had a run in with some timber wolves, these animals were really hungry. They really wanted to attack us and we had to shoot two of them. We drove the others off. Our job was to infiltrate the 10th Mountaineers command post; they said it could not be done. We got by their sentry, and as soon as it got dark, we saw by their campfire that the colonel was alone. So at the opportune time we snatched him, and their colors, and choppered back to our CP with him bound and gagged. We treated this sergeant (war game "colonel") really rough, we told him we would throw him out of the bird if he didn't give us the information we needed. In Vietnam, throwing VC out of a bird at 1000 feet was everyday stuff to get them to give information. One time in 1964 we threw out 6 VC who were bad asses in general. After we threw out the six of them, the other two talked their heads off as to where there were more Victor Charlie battalions hidden and where their supply lines were.

To deal with the Communists was like dealing with snakes. Most of the Special Forces people in our units were Vietnam Vets. We went into International Falls, Minnesota. After being out in the cold for three weeks, we got a motel and six cases of Canadian Mist Whiskey for two days. We met some live wire girls at some of the bars. These girls were just itching to break the boredom. So we rented 16 rooms and the party started. All the women could talk about was, "Gee, you guys are really Green Beret Special Forces, paratroopers, rangers, frog men, demolition experts, karate experts, etc...?"

The motel called the local police and we were told to keep the noise to a low roar. Well, our staff sergeant in charge told them to go to hell! So they pulled a gun on him and arrested him, but the CO got him out the next day and we left.

This time they had a big formation at Meade for us, because we had performed so well by capturing a Colonel and their colors. So everyone was handed out three days leave. I went down and saw uncle Mike, he said, "I hear you are now a dog face soldier, well, Gator, anything you're good at, do it." Mike had worked at Peoples Drug Store in Washington, D.C., for years and then he worked in Virginia for Peoples Drug Store for ages. He said he always liked the way a drug store smelled. Mike had a black cocker spaniel poodle called Ja Ja. We would sometimes call her Gee Gee and Mike used to take her with him in his car. She was a real watch dog. She also slept at the foot of his bed. She lived to be 16 years old. If she was in the car and she didn't know you, you better not touch the windows. When she died, he buried her in the backyard. I stayed at Mike's a lot. He was more a father to me than my own father.

Chapter 10

This was January, and the Army was doing some big things, such as increasing their forces. We were again used as an aggressor force, this time in Brazil, more hot weather and even headhunters to contend with. And talk about snakes and crocodiles!

The Amazon river was a death trap, put your fingers in the water and presto! No fingers.

There is a certain little fish that looks like our sunfish, but they're called piranha and they are like the resident crocodiles. They would go for you in a second. We had three men eaten alive by an overturned LRC (light rubber craft) accident. The piranha and the crocodiles must have made a deal not to eat each other, because they owned the river and surrounding water areas together.

A week before, we had done a HALO (high altitude low opening) free fall into some of the wildest wilderness jungle one would ever hope to lay eyes on. We had to make 11 check points on this operation within a certain time frame and out again. We had para-dropped all our equipment, rubber boots, food, and other gear by C-130 with 6 jumpers following the gear in. The rest of us HALOed our way in. When we met up and set up our camp, we realized we weren't alone. From the bushes nearby we spied a lone naked man, with a bow and a quiver of arrows. He was watching us from a prone position. We hadn't seen anything of the troops we were supposed to be aggressing.

At the same time I saw an anaconda on a tree limb just waiting to drop on us. As we pulled under the limb, we M-79 blooped it: no more head on the snake. Our strange visitor hauled ass when he saw the explosion in the tree limbs. We were navigating by compass and some of this country had never seen civilization before. We returned to camp and on the way through the underbrush we made a gristly discovery. There we found six or seven shrunken heads on some poles. They had been put there some days before, but the heads resembled GI heads and features. Talk about being shook in your boots. Everyone set up double security, claymore mines, and tripwires. This was not on the agenda. We were in the headhunters' backyard. We hung com wire with rocks in cans, so we could hear them also that night. We heard a can with a rock make the warning noise we had set into a perimeter. So we formed a 360 for defense.

About dusk, and sure enough around 2330 here they came, we popped clay mores and threw grenades at them or in their attacking directions. We had not at first known that they had silently scaled trees, because the monkeys and parrots and other birds did not seem to be excited. As the attack raged on, we were being killed by poison arrows and spears. We had two M-60 guns with rifle fire, and we stopped their onslaught. We were attacked every 20 minutes. By morning light we had seven dead, no one survived the poison darts, arrows, and spears.

We were on the radio, PRC-25 radios are very powerful in the right places, we called in for pick up support, we found that the other forces that we were supposed to oppose had been attacked also. This was headhunter savage country, they had also taken a lot of casualties. We got in the big evacuation choppers and loaded our dead and gear. We must have killed around 75 of them, they were painted in different colors and were bare footed, with very long hair. Some of them even had shrunken skulls around their waists. They also had attacked us with machetes. There was about 3 of them that got inside our 360 that we killed up close.

This was the last time, I think, that our Armed Forces ever sent troops into this Amazon country. These people did not take kindly to strangers entering their domain. Our leaders told us to keep silent about this, but I figure we should pay tribute to the brave men who died there. As we flew out of there, we saw more of them coming in boats paddling as fast as they could. The local residents through an interpreter from a town nearby said it was sure death to enter there. They told us some stories about people who had paddled or walked into there and were never seen or heard from again. A very scary thought. Well, I am sure no one else was ever jumped in there again. When we made our report, the SF Commander said, "You handled this as best you could, no one had given thought to the existence of cannibals and headhunters." We were told to chalk it up to good training. My one last thought was these people must be really hungry for revenge, and we were lucky we were well armed. Even with a small unit you can hold off some terrible attacks if you got the ammo to fight with. Also we learned all the tactics the hard way in Vietnam. So in a way it was a scene from Vietnam all over again. We got into Homestead Florida AFB, and the dead were taken off. I knew three of them well.

Well, when we got home to Fort Meade, everyone was wanting to know what the hell happened. Of course, in a very short order the whole post knew it was the talk of the town, even Fort Brag found out we had been on a live-fire mission and lost some people. Some orders came in to split up the units, and attach everyone out to different infantry outfits, so our team was sent to North Carolina to assist in a massive parachute jump. These mass jumps are dangerous because sometimes as you are descending you are directly over another canopy and you find yourself walking that canopy, and the canopy below steals your air and collapses you. At that low height it's too low to pull your reserve, so you walk right off that canopy and jump to one side, so you can stay open. I had even went through somebody else's suspension lines and was hung up until we landed together in a heap. You can get hurt bad that way. When your head or any part of your body makes contact first, it's as bad as having a suspension line caught over your canopy and creating a Mae West effect. Your canopy looks like two large breasts, and brother, you better shake out that reserve; a Mae West canopy will make you drop like a rock.

I was doing a lot of jump master work, and we as a unit were engaged in a lot of repelling mountain climbing, especially around Dahlonega, Georgia. Here is where they make you a mountain climber, and when you are repelling at night, it can get a little hairy. You soon get to be an expert at what you're doing, your life and others depend on scaling in unison and silently. Well, after we finished our mountain leadership refresher course, we did some ranger training refresher courses. "Keep sharp" is the motto.

We trained on all phases at all times. The only way to keep good at what you're doing is to keep practicing when you are a jump master. It is your job to put your guys on the spot where they're needed and this is why, before you jump a stick of men or a team of four, you generally use a wind dummy. A wind dummy lets the pilots and jump master know what direction the wind is in, and generally how many knots of ground wind is blowing on the ground. You wouldn't want to put jumpers in jeopardy for no good reason, especially training jumps. A wind dummy is a straw stuffed clown-looking object that is on the same size level as the average paratrooper and weighs about the same. Some outfits use a boxer's heavy punching bag—it serves the same purpose. Jump mastering is an art. A good jump master can save a lot of lives, really put his men in the right spot, at the right time, especially in a combat situation, and especially in dangerous terrain or over water.

I remember once we were on patrol and it was really Indian country. We noticed a large group of NVA on both sides of a road. This was south of Hoi An, Vietnam. We had a Marine crawl down a low spot and shoot two 45 pistols off in both directions. At this time the NVA started killing each other off. We laughed our asses off as they continued to shoot at each other all night long. It was almost like they were determined to wipe each other out. In the morning they must have been really surprised that they had been killing each other all night. With tremendous casualties, it wasn't too many times that we outwitted them that well. We have to remember one thing: we were always in their backyard. Our Congress was not backing up our policies to win an all-out war; we were pawns and we made the sacrifices. We will never forget that.

If the government had not been so scared of China intervening, we would have made Vietnam the 51st State. The way it was, we did our job and did it well. Another thing, when they brought the M-16 rifle to do combat with, a lot of people died because of needless malfunctions. If the military would have stayed with the M-14 rifle, at least people would have had a fighting chance. The M-16 and its 222-caliber was constantly deflecting off of underbrush and missing the intended enemy. I saw with my own eyes men who were killed or captured because of malfunctions. I witnessed a shell that failed to eject in an M-16; the man was killed because his rifle couldn't fire. When you really needed a weapon, you were stuck with that piece of undependable shit. I was lucky we had the M-14 rifle and an M-60 machine gun which, outside of losing your barrel some-times, had a nasty habit of the barrel locking-lever latch raising up, and the barrel would fall off. I know not where. If the gunner watched out for this, the M-60 was the best. So the word was, you can't fire them without the barrel. So we used to keep the barrel locking-lever latch on the M-60 tied down with com wire.

For all-around 100% satisfaction, my other famous life saver was the 45 pistol. One night I was awakened out of a dead sleep and killed six enemies with that tried and true pistol. I never slept without a loaded 45 in my near grasp. Since 1911 it has gone down in history that it always performed under the worst circumstances, in an elegant manner. Our other man killer was the famous entrenching tool. When you screwed down the bladed shovel part to half-open it would make a terrific head chopper in up-close combat. It was nicknamed the E-tool. The famous battle cry was "half mast the E-tools!" when hand-to-hand combat was near. Once when our outfit had dug in on a ridge, we noticed Charlie coming in under his own artillery umbrella. It was sure death for them, but they hoped to surprise us with this tactic which they had used against the French so well. One thing about all this—the NVA had the experience. First they fought the Japanese, then the French, and then us.

Well, to get back to our Special Forces outfit in the Spring of 1980, our team—with several other teams—were doing a HALO off the tailgate of a C-130. The weather was really cold, and we were jumping Pendleton drop zone Oceana, Virginia. Well, sir, it was a night jump and we all landed on barbed wire, buildings, roofs, etc.. I hit a water tower. The wind blew me right over the railing tower. I felt a smarting sensation on my left heel. I fell practically 100 feet with a half-opened chute. When I hit the ground, I couldn't walk without a limp. They x-rayed me at Fort Meade. The dispensary at the VA Hospital in D.C. misread the the x-ray. If it's not broke, don't fix it, but I had a hairline fracture and they didn't detect it until I was back on full duty again. Well, I ran around on that fracture for one day, and they had me x-rayed again. It was a hairline fracture on the lower left arch, resulting from a parachute jump into a high water tower and bouncing off a building wall before making contact with the ground. So I now would be in a cast up to my knee. Only a week late. I received a pair of crutches and got in my car and drove home. These old legs of mine have been hurt so many times, I dare not count. This was the spring of 1980.

My enlistment was up in June 1980, so I went back to Fort Lee, Virginia, and became an instructor on overseeing parachute equipment. I had a few months left to go on enlistment. So what's a better way? We oversaw everything that slides down the packing tables. The new people who wanted to be parachute riggers started from scratch. They were taught how to use a sewing machine and the correct stitches. In general they learned to manufacture the whole T-10 chute, harness, nylon, suspension line material webbing buckles, D rings, and the reserve chute. They packed and jumped it also. We had everything under the parachute loft, from the largest cargo chutes to the T-10 chutes. When a parachute or reserve chute has had the once-over and been packed, it's signed by the man who packed or repaired it. The white reserve emergency chute was 28 feet wide, compared to the regular nylon 32 footer. All in all, working as a rigger was fun. There was a sign above the parachute supply distribution hatch. It said, "If your last chute didn't open, bring it back and we'll give you another."

While at Fort Lee, Virginia, we had parachute riggers from all branches of the services, including many different countries. One thing we all had in common was to create the best jumping parachute in the universe with little or no chance for any malfunctions. The main malfunctions are the men and women who jump. Some people don't watch their body positions going off a ramp, tailgate, or side door in aircraft and it can be very dangerous not to use proper body positions. One thing to bear in mind, no matter how well the chutes are packed, a bad body position can screw things into a Mae West suspension line caught over a canopy, or worse, a canopy which is completely inverted, which means you have to get out the reserve properly while falling and throw your reserve canopy away from you, so it does not get entangled with your other chute. I cannot advise you further, because it's up to the average trolley car trooper to follow procedure to the letter.

Fort Lee, Virginia, was great duty, eight-to-five hours, always a party every night, and plenty of excitement during working hours, such as overseeing new cargo, tank, jeep, etc., drops; training new people to be the best. There's another old saying, "Don't worry about what is on your back, worry about your plan of attack." I would drive from Fort Lee, Virginia, to Greenbelt, Maryland, every weekend. I got the cast off and my foot seemed fine except the swelling. Well, with as much trauma as the leg had caught in a short lifetime, I figured another accident I could surely handle, so I went on with the routine.

I was up for promotion to staff sergeant and I had to take a physical first. The doctors said, "You are in bad shape with that left ankle, you have had a lot of trauma; gunshot wounds, a spur removed, two fractures, a shrapnel wound, breaking the left femur. Now this plus being on jump status for four years has given your body a terrible pounding." These were all leg (non-jumpers) doctors talking, so I did not pay much attention to them.

I went up the chain of command and talked to the airborne jump surgeon, who gave me a complete going over with the fine tooth comb and here is what he said: "You are a prime candidate for chronic thrombophlebitis. You could come down with this problem at any period in your career. Thrombophlebitis is sometimes referred to as the Richard M. Nixon malady." Well my brain told me I felt fine. They then said, "We can use a man of your experience and skills in other fields, but the Army will have to train you for something new." I thought, "Yes, Sir," to myself, probably riding a desk and jumping out of chairs. Well, my office expertise was nil or next to nil, as you the reader can see. I was good for just about one thing. Now no prolonged standing, no heavy running, no more jumping out of aircraft while in flight. My options were getting very limited. They almost told me to walk with a cane. As a matter of fact, they did suggest that. I was down to a month, so I decided to look into their options. I only had seven years to retire at least an E-8 rank, but all of a sudden my then wife Ruth suggested a financial career because her employer needed a manager. So we founded a company called Financial Research Inc. in Greenbelt, Maryland. When it came time to reenlist, I could have taken an easy job where a person can sit a lot, but no, stupid me, I turned it down and accepted an honorable discharge.

Chapter 11

In June 1980 we were making a good living in the financial world, nothing to write home about. Doing well and sure enough, 1981 rolls around and I was on a trip returning from Minnesota and I had a blood clot form in the calf of my left leg. By the time I was admitted to the Washington, D.C., VA Hospital, it had entered my lung. I was put on the critical list. They treated me with a clot dissolving drug intravenously. After two weeks I was discharged and put on blood thinning medications, such as were available. I later found out Vitamin E is the best blood thinner available for me.

Well, our business went downhill, because we were drinking a lot and not paying any attention to our clients. It dawned on me that I should have stayed in the Army and retired, but we got the company going upward again. So all was well until 1982 and we divorced.After that I sold the company for a small profit and told my Uncle Mike I was heading west to San Francisco to visit my mother's older sister. She was one year older than Uncle Mike and her health was not good. So I got to California and visited her, but her other in-laws had put her into a nursing home prematurely, mainly her son who was an ex-Marine from Korea. He and I got into a fist fight over his putting his mother in a nursing home, So he could get her house and property. Those kinds of jerks shouldn't be allowed to get away with what he did, but he got a doctor to certify that she was senile and she was not.

Anyway, that is the way life sometimes goes, evil wins over good. She should have changed her will beforehand. Well, like the old saying in 'Nam, "If it moves, shoot it. If it doesn't move, shoot it twice."

I remember when we stormed the prison, out of the corner of my eye I saw about 20 bags of quicklime in a tool shed. I think this was used to destroy the bodies after they were put to death and I also understand they tore the Hanoi Hilton down. They are putting up a shopping center over where it once was. Well, at least I suppose it's their way of hiding evidence, once and for all. These eyes saw when it was there. Also, I got in contact with three of the guys that survived a serious "dust off" (a medical pick-up to evacuate wounded people).

We were returning from patrol and the bird was dropping down to pick us up. Out of the eight of us, only four made it. We couldn't throw the wounded in fast enough, and Joe VC was shooting us up with a 51-caliber M gun, the other four were still alive when the crew chief said, "Enough! We have to fly now." The VC mowed them down, they didn't give them a chance to surrender. It was a heart breaker, but when the crew chief said "Fly!" they flew. Some do, some don't. Some will, some won't. Anyway, we had a reunion. It really felt good to see them again. Thank You, dear Lord, for the many breaks and good luck to keep me hacking it. Pain, you gotta love it!

MILITARY ORDER OF THE PURPLE HEART

CHARTERED BY CONGRESS

1782   1932

3-30-92

Department of Veterans Affairs
Regional Office San Francisco Ca.
Adjudication Division

Unit 2-b

RE: Koski Dale N.

Veteran discovered : he described as the DOG PIT an area where American
soldiers were hung on meat hooks, cut apart with saws, VN people was covered with
blood from doing the work, dismembered heads, arms, personal genitals, testis,
a large hole filled with bones and old flesh. He remembers about 200 plus
bodies. How he got the number we are unaware, if it was just an estimate or
actual count. He reported his discovery to superiors. Since then he believes
there was a cover-up and feels that these may have been MIAs that were not
accounted for.

The Veteran is: nominated for Congressional Medal of Honor, 6 Purple Hearts,
Navy Commendation Combat (V), Silver Star, Combat Action Ribbon, Presidential
Unit Citation, Navy Unit Commendation, Marine Corps Expeditionary Medal,
Vietnamese Service Medal with 5 stars, Vietnamese Campaign Medal with "60" RVN-
MUC-CIVAC and color (1c), Good Conduct with 1s.

Campaigns: included VN Advisory, VN Defense, VN Counter Offensive and VN Counter
Offensive Phase II.

Served: in country of Viet Nam 1963 - 1964, as an advisor and again between 1966
- 1967 in Recon.

Duties: Mainly involved in extensive accounting and patrolling to assist in
gathering combat intelligence. Much emphasis was placed on clandestine methods
of entry into objective areas requiring only the elite reconnaissance team
members.

Thank you for your review of this matter.

Sincerely,

Mike Dormer, NSO, MOPH, (089)

EXCLUSIVELY FOR COMBAT WOUNDED VETERANS

Dale Koski   — Koski, Dale Howard! VA copy

COMBAT HISTORY -EXPEDITIONS-

DATE OF ENTRY	DETAILS	FROM	TO	SIGNATURE
5Mar65	Participated in Cuban Blockade	26Oct62	10Dec 62	
5Mar65	Participated in Vietnam Crisis	25Aug63	16Mar64	
11Apr1966	participated in VIETCONG war I Corps	22Dec 66	15 Jan 67	
25Dec1966	Republic of Vietnam			

Sgt Dale H Koski 1654324 USMC. While participating in a clandestine
Classified,mission operation,was inserted into astrongly fortified, V C
area.Of the northern ICorps area,In the Rep of Vietnam.He and his team
were attempting to,after parachutting,into the area suspected of holding,a group of captured
Airmen;While searching,for the captured men,Sgt Koski,and his men,were subjected to withering
small arms,and machine gun fire,also hand gernade,and relentless,mortar fire,After discovering
that the group of downed flyers,had been tortured,and executed Sgt Koski,was attemping to flee
with one of the american officers,who was still alive.Sgt Dale H.Koski USMC.of the Recon
team,Was struck in the left jaw,the bullet pierced the outer Juglar,on the left side of the
neck,then entered,the mouth below the chin,shattering many teeth,and exited out of the
forehead,At the same time,Sgt Koski,was hit,in the left Fumer leg area.And had shhrapnel
wounds,in botbh lower extremities,of the Ankle areas. in both the right and left
Ankles,and the Buttock areas.He was the only survivor,and was meoved to aa medical
area,Sgt Koski and his team,while stationed at Camp Pendleton,Calif.at the time,originated
from the Las Pulgas area.7th Marine training area.This group who participated in this Heroic
feat,were hand-picked,for thier mission.and were flown from a classified area.Into the
enemy area,From CAMP-PENDLETON, CALIF,Directly in the combat area,This mission was and is
Highly Classified,and has not been divulged.SGT.DALE HOWARD KOSKI 1654324 U.M.C. Was
Awarded his 4th,5th,and 6th Purple Hearts,And so recomended for the Congressional Medal of
Honor. SEC of The NAVY.

BY DIR

AWARDS

DESCRIPTION	STARS, DEVICES	DATE APPROVED	APPROVED BY	DATE MEDAL ISSUED	SIGNATURE
CGMDL	1ST AWD	13May64	IBS, MCS QUANTICO,VA	13May64	
ARMED FORCES EXP.		1JUNE64	H&SCO,IBS QUANTICOVA	17JUNE64	
MARCORPS EXP		19JUNE64	"	22JUNE64	
Vietnam Pre, Unit		29JULY64	"	3AUG 64	
Vietnam EXP		29JULY64	"	3AUG 64	
NAVY COMENDATION/	1				
COMBAT V					
PURPLE HEART			H&S USMC ART VA	8Oct65	
NDSM		30JUNE65	SEC OF NAVY	1 Dec 65	BY DIR
7th Campaign MD		22Oct66	SECNAV		By Dir

KOSKI	DALE	HOWARD	1654324	USMC

KOSKI   DALE   HOWARD

109.

CERTIFIED A TRUE COPY

W. W. WINTER
Captain USMC

CLINICAL RECORD | CONSULTATION SHEET

TO: *Field Hosp Emer*	FROM: (Requesting unit, etc., if activity) 13-0-1 DANANG	DATE OF REQUEST: *Aug 67*

1 Aug 67 Pt was brought into emergency ho with extensive wounds to left jaw-bone. Shell wound in face-neck. Bayonet wound to right calf. Shrapnel in both hands. Left ankle swelling appear fracture. Multiple fragments wounds left ankle. Right ankle conscious oriented ...

Cast put on left ankle multiple ... open wounds multiple wounds ...

2 Aug 67 Pt appear ...

-04-67 Sgt Koski being treated for badly broken left ankle. Recommend ... temp 100+ pulse rapid. ... work up fragment shot wound coming out of face-neck. ... crutches — antibiotics — will ...

04-67 to ...

(over)

IDENTIFICATION (For typed or written entries give: Name, rank, grade; date; hospital or medical facility)

OSKI, DHCL
USMC Sgt. 16 54 324

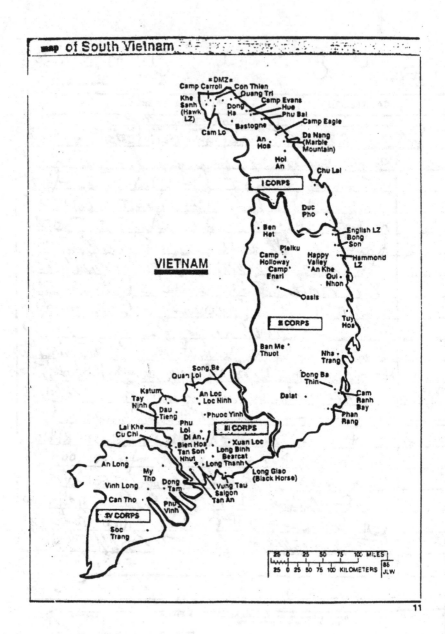

VIETNAM

DMZ
Camp Carroll
Con Thien
Khe Sanh (Hawk LZ)
Quang Tri
Camp Evans
Dong Ha
Hue
Phu Bai
Bastogne
Camp Eagle
Cam Lo
An Hoa
Da Nang (Marble Mountain)
Hoi An
Chu Lai

I CORPS

Duc Pho
Ben Het
English LZ
Bong Son
Pleiku
Happy Valley
Hammond LZ
Camp Holloway
An Khe
Camp Enari
Qui Nhon
Oasis

II CORPS

Tuy Hoa
Ban Me Thuot
Nha Trang
Song Be
Dong Ba Thin
Quan Loi
Katum
An Loc
Loc Ninh
Dalat
Cam Ranh Bay
Tay Ninh
Dau Tieng
Phuoc Vinh
Phan Rang
Lai Khe
Phu Loi
Cu Chi
Di An
Bien Hoa
Xuan Loc
III CORPS
Tan Son Nhut
Long Binh
Bearcat
An Long
Long Thanh
Long Giao (Black Horse)
My Tho
Dong Tam
Vung Tau
Vinh Long
Saigon
Tan An
Can Tho
Phu Vinh
IV CORPS
Soc Trang

25 0 25 50 75 100 MILES
25 0 25 50 75 100 KILOMETERS

11

112.

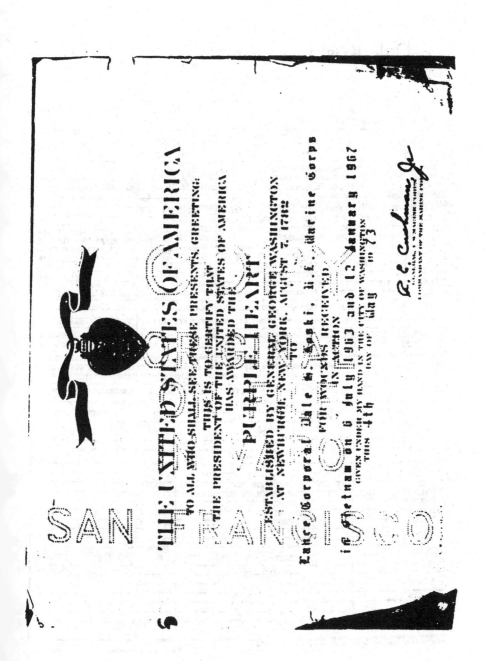

113.

Dale Koski

Koski, Dale Howard! VA copy

COMBAT HISTORY - EXPEDITIONS

DATE OF ENTRY	DETAILS	DATES FROM - TO	SIGNATURE
5Mar65	Participated in Cuban Blockade	26Oct62 20Dec 62	
5Mar65	Participated in Vietnam Crisis	25Aug63 14Mar64	
11Dec1965	Participated VIETCONG near I Corps	22Dec 65 15 Jan 66	
25Dec1966	Republic of Vietnam		

SgtDaleKoski 1654326 USMC.While participating in a clandestine
Classified mission operation,was inserted into astrongly fortified, V C
area.Of the northern Icorps area,in the Rep of Vietnam.He andhis team
were attempting to,after parachutting,into the area,suspected of holding,a group of captured
Airmen,While searching,for the captured men,Sgt Koski,and his men,were subjected to withering
small arms,and machine gun fire,also hand gernade,and relentless,mortar fire.After discovering
that thegroup of downed flyers,had been tortured,and executed,Sgt Koski,was attemping to flee
with one of the american officers,who was still alive.Sgt Dale H.Koski USMC.of the Recon
team,was struck in the left jaw,the bullet pierced the outer Juglar,on the left side of the
neck,then entered,the mouthbelow the chin,shattering many teeth,and exited out of the
forehead.At the same time,Sgt Koski,was hit,in the left Fumer leg area.And had shhrapnel
wounds,in botbh lower extremities,of the Ankle areas. in both the right and left
Ankles,and the Buttock areas.He was the only survivor,and was med ved to an medical
area,Sgt Kos ki and his team,while stationed at Camp Pendleton.Calif.at the time,originated
from the Las Pulgas area.7th Marine training area.This group who participated in this Heroic
fair,were hand picked,for thier mission.and were flown from a classified area.Into the
enemy area.From CAMP-PENDLETON, CALIF;Directly in the combat area,This MISSION was and is
Highly Classified,and has not been divulged. SGT.DALE HOWARD KOSKI 1654326 U.M.C. Was
Awarded his 4th,5th,and 6th Purple Hearts,And so recomended for the Congressional Medal of
Honor. SEC of The NAVY.

BY DIR

AWARDS

DESCRIPTION	STARS, DEVICES	DATE APPROVED	APPROVED BY	DATE MEDAL ISSUED	SIGNATURE
GCMDL	1ST AWD	13May64	IBS,MCS QUANTICO,VA	13May64	
ARMED FORCES EXP.		1JUNE64	HQSCO,IBS QUANTICOVA	17JUNE64	
MARCORPS EXP		19JUNE64		22JUNE64	
Vietnam Pre, Unit		29JULY64		3AUG 64	
Vietnam EXP		29JULY64		3AUG 64	
NAVY COMMENDATION/ COMBAT V					
PURPLE HEART					
NDSM		3OJUNE66	SEC OF NAVY	1) Dc6-66	BYDIR
VI Campaign M2		22Oct66	SECNAV		ByDir

| KOSKI | DALE | HOWARD | 1654326 | USMC |

VH. COPY

DEPARTMENT OF THE ARMY
HEADQUARTERS, FIRST UNITED STATES ARMY
FORT GEORGE G. MEADE, MARYLAND 20755

ORDERS   107-30   AFKA-PA-RED   13 June 1980

[   ]

KOSKI, DALE H.   SGT 11B2Y
3320 S 6th Street   Co B 2d Bn 317 Regt 1 Bde
Arlington, VA 22205   (IN OSUT)(80DIV)(8U3YBO)
                               6901 Telegraph Road
                               Alexandria, VA 22310
                                    ]

You are discharged from component indicated.

Effective date: 26 June 1980
Component: USAR Ready
Type of discharge: Honorable - DD Form 256A
Additional instructions: NA
Format: 500

FOR THE COMMANDER:

DISTRIBUTION: W.E. SCHNUPP
1 - Individual   LTC, GS
1 - AFKA-PA-RED   Asst AG
1 - AFKA-PA-RA (Ref Lib Cy)
1 - CDR, Unit of Assignment
1 - MPRJ

116.

PERSONNEL QUALIFICATION RECORD – PART II

SECTION II – CLASSIFICATION AND ASSIGNMENT DATA

VN COPY

(2) 11B2Y   Team Leader

(1) 11B2X   TEAM LEADER

AWARDS, DECORATIONS & CAMPAIGNS

Ranger
Purple Heart 6
Airborne Wing Scuba-Indo.
(150A10)

Campaigns: VN Advisory/VN Defense/
VN Counter-Offensive/VN Counter-
Offensive Phase IV/

AMERICAN BOARD CERTIFICATION
& LICENSES OR CERTIFICATES HELD

OVERSEA SERVICE
AREA AND COUNTRY

SECTION II — CLASSIFICATION AND ASSIGNMENT

PILOT RATINGS

ORIGINAL	CURRENT
DATE	

PLYING STATUS

INSTRUMENT CERTIFICATION

INTERNSHIPS, RESIDENCIES AND FELLOWSHIPS

HOSPITAL	TYPE OR SERVICE	MONTHS	YEAR

HOSPITAL/TEACHING APPOINTMENTS AND PRIVATE PRACTICE

FROM	THRU	INSTITUTION/LOCATION	TYPE	DURAT
		241		
052044				
70				

CIVILIAN EDUCATION AND MILITARY SCHOOLS

SCHOOL	MAJOR/COURSE/MOSC	DURAT	COMP	YEAR
Cherry Co Elem	General	8Yrs	Yes	'58
USMC	OpenGuerrillaForces		Yes	64
USMC	Sur Evas Resistance			
USMC	to Interrogation &			
	Escape Crs		Yes	65
USMC	Abn Jump Master		Yes	66
USA Inf Sch	Ranger Crs		Yes	66
US Naval Sch	Underwater Swimmer P		Yes	66
USMC	NCO School		Yes	73
USMC	MilFundtnCivilInst		Yes	73
USMC	NCO Ext Crs		Yes	75

APPOINTMENTS AND REDUCTIONS

GRADE	COMP	EFFECTIVE DATE	DATE OF ELIG/RANK
SGT	USAR	780627	

BASIC ENLISTED SERVICE

DATE (BESD) PEBD 680222

TIME LOST (Sec 972, Title 10, USC)

SECTION IV — PERSONAL AND FAMILY DATA

PHYSICAL STATUS		
HEIGHT	WEIGHT	GLASSES
76½	235	

DATE OF EXAM 790617

NUMBER OF DEPENDENTS

ADULT	CHILDREN
	Ø

CITIZENSHIP
SELF Minnesota
SPOUSE Peru

HOME OF RECORD/ADDRESS
HOR: 215 Lakeside Drive #101
GREENBELT, MD 20770

CIVILIAN OCCUPATION

JOB TITLE	DOT CODE
SALES MANAGER	

Dale Hkoski

119.

Re: Dale H. KOSKI; C-23-433-356

Dear Mr. McCormack:

In response to your inquiry about Dale H. KOSKI I desire to assist in his case by providing the following information. I served with Sergeant KOSKI as a member of 2nd Force Reconnaissance Company at Camp Lejeune, NC during 1964, 1965, and early 1966. At this time we were involved in very intense training prior to the Vietnam build-up. It mainly involved extensive scouting and patrolling to assist in gathering combat intelligence. To accomplish this task, much emphasis was placed on clandestine methods of entry into objective areas. The methods of entry were parachuting and swimming. Sergeant Koski was a member of one of these elite reconnaissance teams. Rich in skill, ability, and possessing a spirit of service equal to that of a real professional. Sergeant KOSKI was an inspiration to all that served with him.

I remember Sergeant KOSKI being involved in a parachute accident. I cannot recall the exact date, however I believe it to be late August 1965. Sergeant KOSKI had a malfunction of his main parachute at Mile Hammock Bay drop zone. Sergeant KOSKI was very lucky because he went streaming into the trees that border the Northwest side of that drop zone. He was fortunate in that he hit in the very top of a tall pine tree, feet first. I believe that had it not been for the tree arresting his fall, Sergeant KOSKI may have been killed. I do recall Sergeant KOSKI being hospitalized for a short stay as a result of this incident and walking around the following month with the assistance of crutches.

Although I am not sure of the date of this incident, other data that I mentioned is true and actually did happen. How could one forget an event like that? I hope my statement assists in setting the record straight. Please contact me if I can be of further assistance.

Sincerely,

Charles W. Campbell
Charles W. Campbell
Master Gunnery Sergeant USMC Retired

RECEIVED

JAN 26 1987

AM. LEG. DEPT.

121.

COMBAT HISTORY - EXPEDITIONS - AWARDS RECORD (1070)

COMBAT HISTORY - EXPEDITIONS

DATE OF ENTRY	DETAILS	DATES FROM (ON)	70 -	SIGNATURE

AUTHORIZED AWARDS

NAME OF AWARD	NUMBER OF STARS	DEVICES	DATE MEDAL ISSUED	SIGNATURE
NAVY COM CONV		V	JUL 63	
PURPLE HEART	1		JAN 67	
COMBatAct			DEC 66	
NUC			DEC 66	
GCMDL	1		MAY 67	
USMDEXPD			NOV 62	
MDSM			MAR 61	
PUC			63	
VSM		Fraer	JAN 65	
RVCM	60		OCT 65	
Purple Heart	1 Gold		May 7	
	39 Silver			
Purple Heart				
RVLMUCCivActColor(1C)		Palm	4 414	
GCM	2		750410	

EMBOSSED PLATE IMPRESSION

CERTIFIED A TRUE COPY

W. W. WINTER
Captain USMC

COSKY   DALE

123.

TO: Medical Board Commanding Officer, National VIA: Naval Medical Center Bethesda, Maryland	KOSKI, Dale MARINE BARRACKS, 8TH & I STREETS, WDC 20390 M/CAUC 23 MAY 44

10 00	E5	USMC	0311	battle casualty	Viet Nam

ACTIVE DUTY NAVY   DATE:
ACTIVE DUTY NAVY RECRUIT   PLACE:
ACTIVE DUTY MARCORPS
ACTIVE DUTY MARCORPS RECRUIT
OTHER

DTE-AGGRAVATED BY SERVICE
DTE-NOT AGGRAVATED BY SERVICE
ONSITE

7-460804   2 0 APR 1976   2 0 APR 1976   2 0 APR 1976

REFER TO CENTRAL PEB
DISCHARGE PHYSICAL DISABILITY
DISCHARGE ENLISTED IN ERROR
DISCHARGE CONVENIENCE OF GOVT.

DISCHARGE UNSUITABLE FOR SERVICE
RETURN TO FULL DUTY
RETURN TO LIMITED DUTY
DEPARTMENTAL REVIEW OR OTHER

SIGNED WAIVED RIGHTS
SIGNED WAIVED RIGHTS
WAIVING REBUTTAL

CHRONIC PLANTAR FASCIITIS, RIGHT FOOT,
SYMPTOMATIC #7320

MULTIPLE SHRAPNEL WOUNDS TO LEFT THIGH,
RIGHT HAND, RIGHT THIGH, AND LEFT LOWER
NECK, HEALED. 7090

BAYONET WOUNDS TO LEFT UPPER CHEST AND
RIGHT UPPER QUADRANT, HEALED. 7090

MALARIA, RESOLVED

BOARD MEMBERS	GRADE/CORPS	SERVICE	SIGNATURE
R. K. SLEMONS	CAPT MC	USN	R. K. Slemons
C. W. HARRISON	LCDR MC	USNR	

31. FIRST ENDORSEMENT: DATE: MAY 4 1976

FROM: CONVENING AUTHORITY

TO: Senior Member, Physical Evaluation Board.

VIA:

1. INDICATED DISPOSITION OF THE MEDICAL BOARD IS APPROVED. DISCIPLINARY ACTION OR ADMINISTRATIVE INVOLUNTARY SEPARATION ACTION(S) NOT PENDING.

2. This patient is directed to report to Marine Barracks, 8th & I Streets,
Washington, D. C. to await PEB action.

C. S. LAMBERT
CAPT, MC, USN
By direction

124.

/ 3

MILITARY ORDER OF THE PURPLE HEART
CHARTERED BY CONGRESS

1782   193.

MEMORANDUM

To: Department of Veterans Affairs
        San Francisco Regional Office
        Adjudication Division

        UNIT 212A

                                        May 13, 1992

                                        Re: KOSKI, DALE M.

                                        Claim # 23 433 356

The above captioned veteran has a pending claim in which he is requesting
reevaluation for several conditions including Post-Traumatic Stress Disorder,
Thrombophlebitis, Dental Condition due to gun shot wound in the jaw and Left Leg
fracture.

This service is contending that this attached copy of a consultation sheet SF
513-104-02 dated 1 Jan 67 thru 4 Jan 67 from a field hospital in Da Nang, South
Viet Nam signed by LTJG Cummings, USN/MC clearly supports Mr. Koski's claim for
Dental Trauma, Thrombophlebitis and Left leg fracture. We ask that this evidence
be reconsidered, it is felt that this medical report, that states "MR. KOSKI WAS
BROUGHT INTO EMERGENCY WITH EXTENSIVE WOUNDS TO LEFT JAW - LOSS OF TEETH, WOUNDS
IN FACE AND HEAD - BAYONET WOUNDS TO RIGHT SIDE OF BODY, SHRAPNEL -FRAGS IN BOTH
ANKLES, LEFT ANKLE APPEARS FRACTURED, MULTIPLE FRAGMENT WOUNDS LEFT ANKLE AND
RIGHT ANKLE. TEMPORARY MEDICAL TREATMENT APPLIED - PATIENT IS
CONSCIOUS/CONSIDERABLE LOSS OF BLOOD - TREATMENT X-RAY PROBE" Further down the
page on 1-4-67 it states "SGT KOSKI BEING TREATED FOR BADLY BROKEN LEFT ANKLE
RECOMMEND PINS - TEMP 100 DEGREE PULSE RAPID - SUBSTANTIAL WORK UP FOR GUN SHOT
WOUND COMING OUT OF FOREHEAD", was overlooked and not considered and could be
viewed as new and material evidence for reopening of this claim.

Thank you for your review of this matter.

Sincerely,

Mike Eб

Mike Dornner, NSO, MOPH, (089)

EXCLUSIVELY FOR COMBAT WOUNDED VETERANS

'·ATONA SERVICE OFFICER

M E M O R A N D U M   · 1782   193

TO: Department of Veterans Affairs   Re: KOSKI, DALE H.
       San Francisco Regional Office
       Adjudication Division

UNIT   212A   OPERATION SNAFU   Claim # 23 433 356

FOW MIA'S TRUE STORY

Marine Corps Special Forces, Force RECON and Special Forces,
on a rescue mission, jumped into Hanoi Hilton to free the POW-
MIA. A mission our country will never admit due to the loss of
lives of so many POWs. It is known as :

INCIDENT AT HANOI

Sergeant Dale H. Koski, a Recon Marine, the Elite of the Elite,
tells us what happened in operation snafu. Left for dead, he was
the only survivor in his group. After this mission, Sergeant Koski
was nominated for the Medal of Honor and three Purple Hearts,
in addition to three he already had.

A Recon Marine's courageous story of survival in an enemy terri-
tory.

Devil Dogs.

Sergeant Koski 3rd Marine Division
in May 1967,
Combat Veteran of two
tours in Vietnam.

It is my dream that others will know the story of what
occurred during the Operation. the objective of which was to rescue downed pilots being held
prisoner in the Hanoi Hilton. On December 24, 1966, we jumped into intense. hostile fire from
which I was the only member of my team to survive.

Honorable William J. Clinton
President Of The United States
C/O White House
Pennsylvania Avenue
Washington D.C.   March 8, 1994

Sir:

I wish to take this opportunity to express my opposition to lifting
the embargo with Vietnam especially in light of the atrocity I
witnessed at the Holo Prison, Hanoi Hilton on December 24, 1966.
Members of the 3rd Force Recon Unit, made a low level parachute
jump into the prison. We encountered very stiff resistance.
After we knocked down the front gate of the courtyard, we discovered a dog pit full of vicious dogs and dead prisoners who
were thrown to them to be eaten. Inside the prison itself on
every floor we found freshly killed prisoners. The floor was
slippery with their blood. All we saw were inchained prisoners
hanging from chains.

On the fourth floor we found an American flyer staked out over a
fire being tortured by two Russian torture technicians.

Enclosed is the stressor statement that I submitted to the Dept.
Of Veterans Affairs regarding my part in this operation. I was
awarded my 4th, 5th and 6th Purple Heart and nominated for the
Congressional Medal Of Honor now in the Capable hands of Congress-
woman Nancy Pelosi. If they would look under the Hanoi Hilton,
they would find 250 remains. I was the sole survivor of this
operation. I am trying to enlist your help to bring this atrocity
to light.

In conclusion, my greatest hope is that someday this country will
be run by compassion not greed. American Businessmen and Congressmen
will make millions on lifting the embargo. I am sure the Vietnamese
will not admit this atrocitis nor do I think this is the best way to
settle the POW MIA issue.

I hope this matter will be settled in my lifetime, I am tired of having
nightmares over this operation.

                                        I Remain Your Servant,

                                        Dale H. Koski
                                        Former Sgt. Dale H. Koski
                                        USMC #1654324

P.S.   With your busy schedule, I am sure you will never see this letter.
       My only hope is that this letter is forwarded to somebody with
       enough guts to bring this to light, I feel better and finally rest.

                              Ditto

HANOI HILTON
Atrocities observed by Dale H. Koski

On December 24th 1966 at the Holo Prison, we jumped from a low altitude of 600 feet into a courtyard. We knocked down the front gate with a 3.5 rocket launcher. The first thing we saw was 20 to 30 bags of quick lime in a compartment. On the first cell block of about 35 cells, 12 x 14 feet, 1 or 2 POWs held in shackles in each cell. The POWs were slumped over, shot through the head. The floor was covered with blood and spent AK .47 cartridges cases. There was also a dog pit containing human remains with arms bound behind them. There were at least 4 to 5 vicious dogs, that looked like German Shepherds in the pit mixed with a larger breed.

With other RECON members, we continued up. I saw the something on the next floor. POWs in chains, shot through the head. I also saw POWs in a large room hanging on meat hooks, dismembered people drawn and quartered while still alive. Blood and guts all over the walls and ceiling. There was a living quarter for the guards about 50 yards from the slaughter and carnage rooms. Our RECON members threw frag and WP Grenades in the room and shot several guards who were trying to escape.

As we continued to the 3rd cell block, we encountered hostile machine gun fire. By this time we were encountering brief confrontations of withering gun fire. From the time we landed by parachute, we were subjected to a constant barrage of 51-calibre machine gun fire, AK-47, and SKS fire. We lost almost every member of the Force RECON Black-out Operation group. But those of us who survived continued hand to hand combat and under barrages of enemy gun fire, we pressed on. When we entered a large room off the hallway, we saw a POW stretched over hot coals. He was tied down with his wrist wired to a steel pole and his feet tied the same way on the other end. His flesh subjected to the burning coal. We could smell the burning flesh odor. As we entered we shot at least four Russians and 10 Vietnamese torture technicians wearing leather aprons. These torture technicians were busily engaged in dismembering live POWs with surgical saw. The POWs I saw were hanging on meat hooks through their spine and out the back of their necks. While still alive, these men were bound hand and foot with wire. A Russian was busily interrogating them a the torture went on.

Again, we were subjected to intense enemy fire as we headed down the stairs to the bottom of the cell block. I saw another dog pit with human remains inside. We threw grenades at the dog pit. I observed more corpses hanging on meat hooks, perhaps 250 POWs. The last thing out th door, I saw human bones in a pile. Some corpses still had wire tied around the wrist and feet. M Radioman was killed and I looked around but there were no other troops near me. I got on loading dock, jumped off onto the grass, and there was a wounded POW trying to escape headed t the chopper. I helped him up over my shoulder and ran. We received enemy fire, the POW wa shot dead, and I ran for the chopper. One other Marine, directly behind me was shot down from th back. As I ran toward the chopper which was about 10 feet above ground, I had to jump for it. Th pilot hollered to get on. We were airborne about 9 or 10 minutes and flying constantly throug heavy flak and air burst when we went upside down into three canopy jungle. I was thrown out ar fell around 70 or 100 feet through tree branches. When I hit the ground, I landed into a creek ban its mud broke my fall. I observed one of the pilots hacked to death by Russians and NVA regula with machetes. At this point I evaded and escaped until I was rescued.

Dale H. Koski, former Sgt. 3rd Force Reconnaissance USMC, 16543

Incident At Hanoi   By Sgt. Dale H. (Gator) Koski

Sketched picture of Dale while in the VN Jungle

Bemidji, Mn. May 1944, The day Dale H. Koski was born. During his younger years, he managed to pick up the nick name 'Gator' while living in Florida. Some how the nick name stuck with him since.

Coming from a family who's father and brother served in the Armed Force Dale .became very interested. It was during the early months of 1961, where in Baltimore Maryland he spoke with a recruiter. Shortly after he found himself being flown to Jacksonville Fl, and from there to Parris Island. Over the course of the next few years Dale was trained in specialized combat and survival courses, where he mastered the arts. After the torturous and rigorous training, Koski and the others found they were not only training with the elite, but were training with the elite of the elite.

During the late months of 1962, Dale participated in the Cuban Blockade. From August 1963 to March 1964, he participated in the Vietnam Crisis.

It was Operations and Missions like those which Koski and fellow team members were honored with some of the following awards.

1. *Marine Corps Expeditionary Metal,* 2. *Navy Commendation Metal w/ V,* 3. *Presidential Unit Citation,* 4. *Navy Unit Commendation,* 5. *Three Purple Hearts,* 6. *VSM w/ 5*, 7. *VCM w/ 60.*

It was late December of 1966 when the famous 3rd Force Recon was given a Highly Classified Mission. They were to be inserted into a strong fortified area in the North, the mission was to rescue suspected Airmen being held captive, at a place called Hoa Lo Prison. The Operation was called SNAFU. According to military records, It was on December 24, 1966 the Recon team was inserted into this heavily armed and well defended area. As their parachutes descended from the dark night skies, they began taking on small arms fire, machine gun fire, hand grenades and relentless mortar fire. Many were dead before they hit the ground. Immediately on ground contact, they moved towards the compounds entrance and blew the door .

Hoa Lo Prison

After battling their way through and into the compound they attempted to go from room to room under the intense fire, They eventually made it to the second floor to where the NVA and Russians solders were housed. They found the POWs they had come for had been tortured and executed, They had no other recourse but to return to the pick up point. They found a wounded POW trying to escape. Koski helped him over his shoulder and ran towards the chopper. While under intense gun fire the POW was shot in the head. By that time only Koski and another officer was left. As they ran to the chopper, the officer was shot. His chopper began taking off as Koski jumped and grabbed and hung onto the skid. The pilot hollered to get in. Dale had been hit with the same kill the POW it struck the outer jugular on the left side of the neck then entering the mouth which shattered his chin and teeth, then exiting out his forehead, at the same time he was hit in the left femur as well as shrapnel wounds in both lower extremities of both right and left ankles and buttocks. They then flew for about 9 or 10 minutes through flak and air burst, they could see about 60 trucks w/troop heading down the road. They also witniess some of the vehicle running down some of their own soldiers being chased. They called for F-105s which wasted no time coming in to drop napalms. Suddenly the chopper went upside down into a triple canopy jungle of trees. Uncertain if the pilot died on impact, the co-pilot remained in the burning chopper. Sgt. Koski fell 70 to 100 feet through the limbs and branches of the trees (which was responsible for saving his life) and landed in a creek bank. Russian and NVA regulars were on top of the site in no time. The pilot was quickly hacked to pieces with machetes. This was the start of his journey home. Operation SANFU was a mission specially designed to rescue our POW's in that prison. That prison became to be known "THE HANOI HILTON"

Entrance to Hoa Lo Prison—Before Renovation

The attempt to return and be picked up by friendly was some what like to the Bat 21 rescue in ways, Koski has published his testimony in a book called: "INCIDENT AT HANOI" (Operation Snafu) If you have not read it, you should, The U.S. Government nor the North Vietnamese Government has not outwardly admitted to this operation, because it led to the slaughter of POWs. Yet after this mission he was not only awarded three more Purple Hearts, but was also nominated for the Congressional Metal of Honor.

Several high ranking officers at Chapter, State, and National level of the MOPH have been assisting him in obtaining the status of the C.M.H.

MOPHTEX-VETNEWS

129.

MILITARY ORDER OF THE PURPLE HEART

Commandant of the Marine Corps
Mmrb-10
Headquarters U.S. Marine Corps
Washington, D.C. 20380-0001

Michael G. Thompson
236 Point Lobos Avenue
San Francisco, CA 94121

April 12, 2002

Subject: Inquiry into a Nomination for the Congressional Medal of Honor,
Sergeant Dale H. Koski, USMC Service #: 1654324

Sir,

As adjutant to the Military Order of the Purple Heart (MOPH) here in San Francisco,
California.

I am helping a former marine named Dale H. Koski, service number 1654324 rank was
Sergeant..

Mr. Koski requested his records from the National Record Center, St Louis, Missouri.
On his form 20, he discovered he was nominated for the Congressional Medal of Honor
for his actions in Vietnam in 1966 as a member of 3rd Force Recon.

On a special operation into North Vietnam to rescue prisoners of war (POWs) at the Hua
Lo prison, nicknamed "Hanoi Hilton" by the media, after they jumped in, all they found
was slaughtered prisoners. Sgt Koski's helicopter was shot down and he was wounded
several times. He eventually made his way back to friendly lines where he was debriefe
and hospitalized. We would appreciate it if someone in your office could help us find if
Sergeant Dale H. Koski was in fact awarded the Congressional Medal of Honor (CMH)
as a result of this operation who was code named SNAFU to confuse radio intercept. He
had a "Death Certificate" in his "201 file" which was not true. He says he was the lone
survivor of this operation. If he was awarded the CMH, please advise us. And if he was
not, did he receive a decoration for his brave actions in this special ops???

I was in Vietnam in 1966 with the U.S. Army "long-range recon" (LLRP) patrol and w
had heard of this operation. Hopefully we can bring this affair to resolution and closure.
And give this former Marine his just dues, instead of falling through the cracks again,
like most cases with Vietnam veterans. I myself am a former Marine who served from
1957-1961.

I am thanking you in advance.   With patriotism;

Michael g Thompson

130.

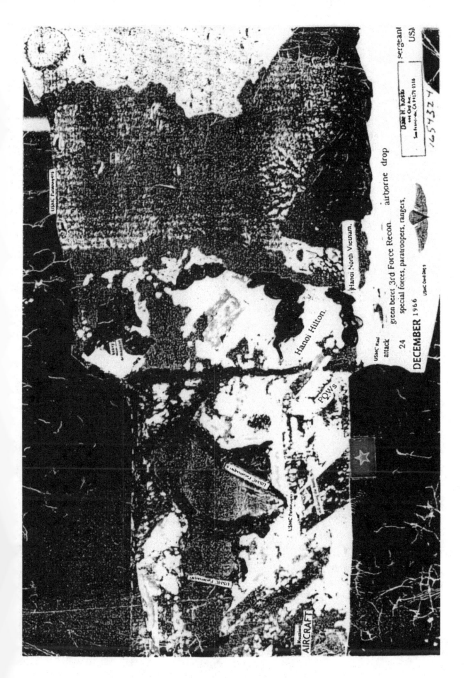

USMC Paratroopers

Hanoi, North Vietnam.

green beret, 3rd Force Recon. airborne drop
special forces, paratroopers, rangers,
24
DECEMBER 1966

Hanoi Hilton.

USMC Red
attack

POWs

Dan N. Kosh
444 Ord Ave.
San Francisco, CA 94176 1316

sergeant
USA

USMC Cool Dog's

USMC Paratroopers

USMC Paratroopers

AIRCRAFT

131.

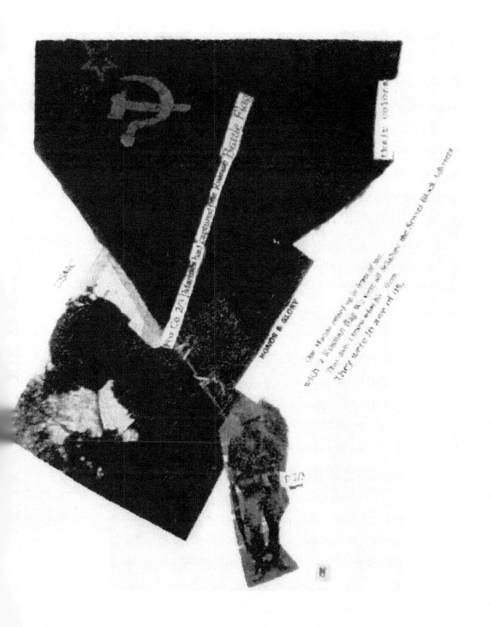

NAVAL REGIONAL MEDICAL CLINIC
Washington Navy Yard Branch
Washington, D. C. 20372

NRMC1:57:LCR;vbs
6120
03 May 1973

From: Senior Medical Officer, Naval Regional Medical Clinic, Washington Navy
Yard Branch, Washington, D. C. 20372

To: Headquarters Marine Corps, Decorations and Medals Branch, Purple Hearts
Section

Subj: KOSKI, Dale LCPL   wounds and medical examination in
the case of

1. LCPL KOSKI has been wounded in the Republic of Vietnam. Wounds received
are as follows:

A. On 05 July 1963 subject member received a through and through
wound in the left foot from a punji stick and a shrapnel wound in the
right leg, as an adviser with Fox Company 2nd Battalion 3rd Marine
Regiment.

B. On 12 January 1967 subject member received four injuries, as the
forward observer with 1st Battalion 3rd Marine Regiment, they are as f:
(1) Shrapnel wounds on forehead above the bridge of the nose
(2) Shrapnel wounds of the jaw, neck and shoulder
(3) Shrapnel wounds of the right hand, wrist and upper arm
(4) Bayonet wound of the right side

2. Medical examination and the subject member's health record verify the
extent of these wounds.

3. If further assistance is required, the undersigned may be contacted at
433 3491.

LT MC USNR
Acting

135.

Printed in the United States
By Bookmasters